Refiguring ENGLISH STUDIES — Refiguring English Studies provides a forum for scholarship on English Studies as a discipline, a profession, and a vocation. To that end, the series publishes historical work that considers the ways in which English Studies has constructed itself and its objects of study; investigations of the relationships among its constituent parts as conceived in both disciplinary and institutional terms; and examinations of the role the discipline has played or should play in the larger society and public policy. In addition, the series seeks to feature studies that, by their form or focus, challenge our notions about how the written "work" of English can or should be done and to feature writings that represent the professional lives of the discipline's members in both traditional and nontraditional settings. The series also includes scholarship that considers the discipline's possible futures or that draws upon work in other disciplines to shed light on developments in English Studies.

Volumes in the Series

David B. Downing, editor, *Changing Classroom Practices: Resources for Literary and Cultural Studies* (1994)

Jed Rasula, *The American Poetry Wax Museum: Reality Effects, 1940–1990* (1995)

James A. Berlin, *Rhetorics, Poetics, and Cultures: Refiguring College English Studies* (1996)

Robin Varnum, *Fencing with Words: A History of Writing Instruction at Amherst College during the Era of Theodore Baird, 1938–1966* (1996)

Jane Maher, *Mina P. Shaughnessy: Her Life and Work* (1997)

Letters for the Living

Teaching Writing in a Violent Age

Michael Blitz
John Jay College of Criminal Justice
City University of New York

C. Mark Hurlbert
Indiana University of Pennsylvania

National Council of Teachers of English
1111 W. Kenyon Road, Urbana, Illinois 61801-1096

Staff Editor: Kurt Austin
Interior Design: Tom Kovacs for TGK Design
Cover Design: Evelyn C. Shapiro

NCTE Stock Number: 28033-3050

Library of Congress Cataloging-in-Publication Data

Blitz, Michael.
    Letters for the living: teaching writing in a violent age/Michael Blitz,
C. Mark Hurlbert.
       p. cm.—(Refiguring English Studies)
    Includes bibliographical references (p.) and index.
    ISBN 0-8141-2803-3 (pbk.)
    1. English language—Rhetoric—Study and teaching—Social aspects—
United States. 2. Report writing—Study and teaching—Social aspects—
United States. 3. Violence—United States. I. Hurlbert, C. Mark. II Title.
III. Series.
PE1405.U6B58   1998
808'.042'071173—dc21   98-13637
                                            CIP

For Mozelle and Terry,
Daina, Roland, Cory, Celine, and René

Contents

Acknowledgments

As with any book, this one reflects a debt to many people. We want to thank, first of all, our students who have shared their time with us in our classrooms and offices, in their writings and projects. Our editor, Michael Greer, provided just the right blend of humor, vision, enthusiasm, patience, and direction to keep us going during a turbulent process. Kurt Austin and Zarina Hock guided our manuscript through the labyrinth. Thanks, also, to Evelyn C. Shapiro and Tom Kovacs for their design work.

We were the grateful recipients of help, advice, encouragement, and friendship from Don Byrd.

A number of our friends, as well as colleagues, and graduate and undergraduate students at John Jay College of Criminal Justice and Indiana University of Pennsylvania have been particularly supportive of our mania over the past few years: Louise Krasniewicz, Gerald Markowitz, Carol Groneman, Jill Norgren, Karen Kaplowitz, Robert Crozier, Abby Stein, P. J. Gibson, Pat LickLider, Serena Nanda, Geoff Fairweather, Don Goodman, Betsy Gitter, the members of TWARC (Teaching the Writing and Reading of Cultures)—David Downing, Don McAndrew, Maurice Kilwein Guevara, Roxann Wheeler, Susan Comfort, Gian Pagnucci, Tom Slater, and Elaine Ware—Rosaly Roffman, Wendy Carse, Dan Collins, Laila El-Omari, Don Pardlow, Deloris Johnson, Immaculee Harushimana, as well as Beth Boquet, Ann Ott, Janine Rider, Carrie Myers, Karen McCullough, Donna Singleton, Gail Tayko, John Tassoni, Jim and Kathy Strickland, Manny Savoupolis, Milagros Vicente, Michele Eodice, Kami Steele, Bob Dandoy, Steve North, Nancy Mack, Jim Zebroski, Elspeth Stuckey, Bill Webster, Kim Ginther Webster, Harrison Fisher, Jane McCafferty, Dan Lowe, Jody Hendrickson, Cal Golay, Jondi Keane, Marge Byrd, and Rabbi Pincus Miller.

No book the two of us write will be without the traces of thought and inspiration of Jim Berlin, whose work in composition and cultural studies opened doors of imagination for us all.

1 Strangers

No more pretending. This is about the living. We don't know who you are. Can we tell you a story? We are teachers of writing. We want to change the world. You already know this story. You are in this story. We think you wrote this story with us. Here's how it goes:

We want to change the world.
We're supposed to change the world.
No one can change the world.
Our students must go "out" and change the world.
Our children will change the world.
Having children and teaching others
has already changed our world.
It's too hard to change the world.
Education should change the world.
We must get out of the way so those who can will change the world.
The wrong people are changing the world.
We are among those who are changing the world.
It's too late to change the world.
It's too early to stop changing the world.

Ours is a society that tolerates violence more and more as a natural part of life and sees peace more and more as an abstraction. The teaching of writing is connected to living. Not living in the abstract, but *living*—and *dying*.

What do we find out about living when we read and discuss our students' compositions or when we examine our own? What do we find out about dying? We find that our students face deaths of all kinds—every day—of the body, of spirit, of hope, of desire, of the ability to care. When we address some of the struggles just to live that our students face, we also address the tensions that tear at the health of the world. It is time to ask ourselves: as teachers of composition, are we prepared for the truly powerful stories our students are ready to tell?

We are going to have to be willing to face the truth that our students are not only among the living but also among the dying, and, like it or not, we are fully in the presence of both.

1

Everything counts. We aren't going to pretend our lives can be withheld in brackets any more than our students can. What is at stake in teaching is the people in the room. The composing of the works. The living that becomes the works. Together. Compositions aren't merely warm-up exercises for the living. Writing and living and teaching are not separable. As you will see, our lives are in *this* composition as our students' lives are in their compositions. Our thinking about teaching, about the poetics of teaching, about the poetry of living, about our students, about our lives, has been intertwined with our writing, especially in our letters to each other. For years we have written to each other every day, primarily in the form of e-mail. We have exchanged fears and a few success stories; we have written to each other about our everyday lives in—and out of—our classrooms, our uncertainties, our syllabi, book choices, life choices, and many, many mistakes. We have reported moments that have frozen us and those that have felt like revelations. Our students have been doing all of this, as well—writing, talking, exchanging successes and failures, dreams, plans, choices—in compositions as varied as the lives that compose them. And now what do we do? What are we to make of all this exchanging and dreaming and making and unmaking of the world? What we are proposing here is that we begin by *looking* at them, honestly, respectfully, usefully.

Some years ago, we participated in a symposium sponsored by the Society for Critical Exchange entitled "Problems of Affirmation in Cultural Theory."[1] At one point, J. Elspeth Stuckey noted that teachers do a lot of talking about the way things ought to be, but that we rarely talk candidly about who we really are, where we really come from, what we've really done in our "secret lives" away from, and before we ever got to, our schools, colleges, and universities. She wondered out loud whether we all thought these "private" matters weren't relevant to our everyday work as educators. In other words, she was suggesting that we might all be pretending. *Letters for the Living* tells real stories about students' lives and our lives, in crisis, in health, in confusion, in success, in sadness, even in rare moments of clarity. How can we best take up Stuckey's challenge to stop pretending that our real lives are secondary or irrelevant to the work of teaching? How can we make these stories, these "private matters," integral to creative, collaborative pedagogy? And how can we best involve our students in shared, collective projects that offer at least one less lonely, less overwhelming way for students to seek relevance for themselves?

We can't imagine why anyone would choose teaching as a profession unless he or she had a notion that educating people is somehow involved in making better neighborhoods, better communities, a better world.

Yet, if educators everywhere are teaching and conducting research toward the understanding and remaking of culture and society, why are our culture and society so chronically unhealthy? Why are our children inheriting a desperately polluted planet, an outrageously unbalanced global economy, dramatically intensified racism, sexism, homophobia, urban squalor, a booming prison industry, mass media aimed at dulling preadolescent intellects, elected officials who have decided that it is more cost effective to allow a rise in poverty and homelessness than to make a commitment to schools and training and long-range socioeconomic justice? What are the crucial differences between what we think we are doing in higher education and what we really are and are not doing? Are we creating anything of value? Value to whom? Do we make things? For whom? Do we make things happen? Do we prevent things from happening? Do we know what we're doing?

Are these the right questions?

———————————

Mark:[2]

Our last conversation about structuring the book as a gathering of e-mail in which we "come clean" about "real life" as composition teachers has made me think about what's at stake in such an effort. So many of my students, here at John Jay College [of Criminal Justice, City University of New York], come from housing projects, high-crime neighborhoods, treeless, glass-littered streets without lights, without security; some students come from sections of New York City in which they will have seen the commission of a major crime on their way to school. Some have been victimized before they've gotten to the subway. Many have told me about home lives that seem even more hostile than the streets. Quite a few have spent years waiting (or not waiting) for a parent or brother or sister to be released from prison. Too many (one is too many) have had to be called upon to identify the body of a loved one who had been murdered.

On the flip side, a number of John Jay College students are in Law Enforcement (Police, Corrections, Armed Security). They often come to school having just gotten off a shift. Many of them tell stories of having to break up brutal knife fights; investigate a murder; discover an abandoned infant in a dumpster; arrest someone and walk, with the perpetrator, through a throng of people who may be furious, in general, with anyone in law enforcement; to arrest children caught with narcotics and/or weapons, sometimes finding the syringe still dangling from a twelve-year-old arm.

Those who have made it through these preposterous situations and have come to college now face unbearable hikes in tuition and fees at this public university. They see their education—their hopes and idealism (tenacious though such idealism must be) kicked out from under them by a governor and mayor who, in a staggering lack of vision, have determined that the City University will work better if the poor cannot afford to attend. Those who do attend must borrow sums of money they cannot hope to repay if they remain in a city whose political and social economy precludes their finding sufficiently gainful employment (let alone in a nation whose leaders are *debating* whether to raise the ridiculously low minimum wage a few cents!).[3] All the odds seem stacked against these students.

But maybe I'm being overly dramatic? Maybe all students face stacked odds in these times. What kinds of odds were (and are) stacked against us? And what about students and teachers whose lives have been relatively comfort- able? You know, the ones that Jim Berlin used to worry about telling that they aren't headed for the good life, the ones who are so comfortable, as Steve North and Cy Knoblauch noted in *Composition and Resistance*, that it is potentially absurd to see them as suffering (125). bell hooks says, "When education is the practice of freedom, students are not the only ones who are asked to share, to confess. Engaged pedagogy does not seek simply to empower students. Any classroom that employs a holistic model of learning will also be a place where teachers grow . . ." (21). Are we growing? You and I, our profession, our colleagues, our society? Sometimes I just don't know.

Michael

_____

MIchael:

There are thousands of comfortable students and teachers. They may find our work ridiculous. Who knows? But there are thousands and thousands (we've met so many of them at 4Cs and NCTE and MLA and in our travels) of teachers and students who have come to our schools and classrooms in the thick of tremendous difficulties. They come to these places to find something, to do something, to form communities, sometimes to escape their communi- ties.

Your students must find ways to survive the streets of New York City; mine must overcome what they tell me about the boredom, alcoholism, violence, and hopelessness of small town, rust-belt living. In the ten years I have been teaching here in Western Pennsylvania, I have noticed a distinct difference in my students. Whereas they used to talk about the future in terms of "having it all," more and more often students begin such discussions by saying, "Well, when I graduate, *if* I can get a job, I will. . . ." These students carry the hopes and dreams of their families with them, both as sources of strength and pressure. We can learn a lot about bravery and survival from our students.

Mark

_____

Every day, our students come in off the streets or come out from the relative safety of their homes. They may leave their kids for a day or take time out from their jobs so that they can be in our classes. And what do they do in those classes? They compose writings from the raw materials of their lives. They examine their lives in ways that may be uncomfortable. They consider the lives and works of others in the context of the experiences that have shaped their own thoughts and actions. We're asking them to put their lives, the way they live their lives, the way they interact with others, into print so that it is available for community discussion and critique—and also for evaluation. And even if we do not ask for this, this is, nonetheless, precisely what happens.

Michael:

I have been reading a book entitled *Schools, Violence, and Society*, a 1996 collection of essays by educators about the complexity of the issue of violence, the effects of violence, drugs, and gangs on the school, and educational programs for countering the growth of violence in our culture. As I read this book, I am once again discouraged by the number of violent incidents in schools:

> Seventy-five percent of all students surveyed reported seeing or hearing about racially or religiously motivated confrontations on a regular basis, up from 57 percent in the 1990 Lou Harris survey. This trend is particularly disturbing in light of the fact that America is becoming more, not less pluralistic. (Futrell 11)

> The suicide rate among teens has quadrupled in the last decade. (Derkson and Strasburger 67)

> Homicide is the twelfth leading cause of death in America, the second leading cause of death for teenagers and young adults, and the leading cause of death for African-American teenagers and young adults fifteen to thirty-four. More than twenty thousand people die each year from homicide, hundreds of thousands are injured by assault, millions are fearful of the risks and potential destruction of intentional injury. (Prothrow-Smith and Quaday 153)

And reporting from a Lou Harris study, Jennifer C. Friday reveals this statistic:

> . . . 62 percent of central city young people reported that they could get a gun, compared with 58 percent of suburban and 56 percent of small-town and rural students. Seventeen percent of students in the central city schools carried a handgun in the past thirty days, compared with 15 percent of suburban students. (25)

An army of children from all corners of the United States.

Although the educators in this book are writing mostly about grade and high school experience, our students were, in many instances, these students just one year earlier. Why on earth would we suppose that the impulses toward, and the scars of, violence go away so quickly, so easily?

I am at this minute remembering an IUP student from several years ago who told me that he carried a handgun wherever he went, even to class—I also remember that he was having real tension with an ex-girlfriend in the same class. Knowing what I know now, I think I would take steps to get him out of my room.

Mark

Mark:

How did you respond to that student telling you he carried a gun? What should you have done? A number of my students are police officers, and, strange as it may sound, I'm more or less used to a proportion of my students being well armed! But I suppose if a civilian student were to tell me what he told you, I'd want to at least tell him that if he is carrying a weapon, he is endangering others who are under my supervision (not to mention endangering me, as well), and that I feel responsible for the safety of those others. For that reason, if not also for legal reasons (if the weapon is concealed and/or unlicensed, he is obviously breaking the law), I cannot keep his gun a secret.

My 101 students came up with a sentence with which they would all begin an in-class writing: "What's wrong with this picture?" They wrote for nearly 25 minutes and didn't want to stop. They will have a chance to work further on this piece over the weekend and have agreed that it will be a major paper of the semester. And I have to tell you, this worries me. It's nothing new to fret over having to grade my students' writing. But the things they wrote about, so far, make me feel particularly reluctant. One student wrote:

> What's wrong with this picture? An eighteen year old kid comes home to find his mother totally drunk, as usual. His little sister has most of her clothes off with her boyfriend who is older and bigger than the eighteen year old so what can he say? The father? Well he's no place, nobody knows where he is or if he is dead. The eighteen year old finds a pile of dirty dishes and empty bottles and the baby brother is crawling around in garbage. So the eighteen year old picks up the baby and puts him in his chair while he starts to clean up the kitchen and make dinner. Nobody's going to eat anyway. The eighteen year old will be too tired to study again and he won't have time to write his paper for the only class he thinks he can do good in. What's wrong with this picture? [4]

Mark, this paper's theme isn't the exception.

Michael

_____

Michael:

Your last posting is heartbreaking. But your student has been able to write about his life, to you, for himself. You cannot underestimate either the significance or the value of this. More and more it seems that much of what we do— or ought to do—as composition teachers is to create respectful spaces for students to tell others who they are. In *"My Trouble Is My English": Asian Students and the American Dream*, Danling Fu writes of four immigrant students: "These four youngsters have many stories to tell, but they have few chances to tell their stories in their school experiences. As a result, they remain strange to others and sometimes even to themselves" (17). I can think of no greater reason to take or teach a composition class than to go about the process of composing in order to become less strange to one's self and others.[5] You know how I bristle when I hear educators refer to composition as a "service course" for the university. I think that composition courses should first be designed to serve our students by helping them to address the important epistemological, political, and cultural needs of their and our day— as you have begun to do in the class activity you just described to me. This is, secondarily, the greatest service we can perform for the college or university.

Michael, your student's piece shows how economics impact on our students' composing and creating. That is worth getting at with him and the other students in our classrooms. That is knowledge that might allow us to come to terms with the lives we lead. As a teacher of writing, I know you know the value of coming to terms—it is no less than the wresting of some sort of control back—from what or whom? Perhaps the very forces and structures that make us strange to ourselves. Perhaps the very people who benefit from our remaining strange even to ourselves—a place from which no useful sense of agency will emerge. I think I know why—or at least am realizing why in a new and restored sense as I write this letter to you—one reason I am so unnerved by the sense of remaining strange. As long as we remain strange, we are also estranged from the strength we need to act in uncomfortable circumstances, the possibility of composing—a frightening thought. As long as we remain strange to ourselves and to others, we remain incapable of forming the kinds of intimacy that can make a social whole possible. The fact is that even though your student has so poignantly written about what is wrong with this picture, your letter has created a stunning portrait of what is right—he is in your class and he is offering a truth of his life for investigation. Can he see the potential in this? Does it mean anything to him? I guess so because he is, despite the odds, in your class.

Now I do not propose to say that your student's life problems are solved by the act of writing a piece entitled "What's Wrong with This Picture?" What I am saying is that in the act of composing this piece, your student is making a space for sharing his difficult situation so that students and you can help him see how it and he are not strange, but all-too-common and connected to larger social realities. Perhaps these connections are worthy of group study in hopes of making some kind of common understanding, some sense of common pain and purpose, some sort of peace, however momentary these things often are.

Mark

Who are these people whose writings are the most vivid cultural studies texts we know? They are someone's child, someone's mother or father, sister, brother, lover, baby-sitter, friend, stranger. Strangers—trying not to be strange. And we're trying to figure out how not to be so strange to them. It's strange to write something to strangers hoping that writing can change that. We are asking our students to write something that will change them and to change readers they may not, in theory, ever know. Hardly anything changes, yet we've been promising change. We read books for change. We call for change, demand change, plead for change. We ask strangers to consider changing everything. We ask strangers to say something to change our minds. Robert Kelly writes, "Wood/of change/to range/me/through" (222). He's longing to change a lifetime by *saying* so. But he recognizes that the wood of change, the material of change is the size of a lifetime. That is, if we want to change the world, it's a lifetime project that begins now. No one can afford to pretend to be outside the range of the project.

Can we say that our pedagogies are not about expressivist writing or about entrance to the academy but about learning how to live?

During the winter of 1993–94, with a couple of feet of snow on the ground, Michael stepped out of his Brooklyn, New York, apartment and began the walk to the subway. His new upstairs neighbor, with whom he had spoken only once, leaned out her window into the icy air and called, "Have a good teach!" She had a great big smile as though she were pleased that, like postal workers, college professors deliver regardless of the weather. The handful of students who made it to John Jay College in Manhattan that day all seemed proud of their own arrival and genuinely pleased to be able to gather in a close circle to present their work or to discuss Sophocles and the question of justice.

Mark:

As I looked around at those dozen or so students, each with a bit of writing about Oedipus or about laws that govern us whether or not we ever understand them, I felt deeply satisfied that they had done the hardest work of all: they'd come together (one from her shift as an undercover narcotics officer, another from one of the most disadvantaged housing projects in the city, and another from dropping her two-year-old daughter off at day care fifty-some-odd blocks away) for a couple of hours to listen to each other and to take and give pleasure in their learning. Maybe this is painfully corny to say, but I was moved.

Michael

We intend *Letters for the Living* as the opening of a window. An occasion to write, to look outside, to peek inside, to call out to our neighbors and friends and, sure, to call out to those with whom we do not agree.

Michael:

The other day, I asked my forty-seven Humanities Literature students what we had learned in this class. They said things like, "we're learning how to read," "we're learning how to talk in a large group," "we're learning how to write and share journals," "we're making friends," "we're learning about our world and American society"—in other words, everything they said had more to do with what they were doing and experiencing than with what they were studying.

Mark

What is it that brings us and our students back to the classroom every day? Many things, but none more important than two: violence and peace. In at least one important sense, we come to find—and to make—peace with ourselves, with others, with a troubled world.

At a fraternity house at Indiana University of Pennsylvania, where Mark teaches, a twenty-one-year-old fraternity brother "came home shortly before 3 a.m. . . . after a night of drinking" (Roddy A-1). He went to the refrigerator to get a sandwich he had placed there the night before. The sandwich was gone. The student produced a 9mm pistol and started to wave it around at the fraternity brothers who were still awake. He then turned to a target tacked to a wall, a silhouette of a human being. He shot the pistol. The bullet went through the wall and struck his sleeping roommate. When the student realized what he had done, he became distraught, put the gun to his own head, and killed himself. After sending the wounded roommate to the hospital, the police obtained a search warrant and removed eight more guns, including rifles, from the frat house.

This dead young man, too, was someone's student, not to mention someone's son or brother.

The Pittsburgh Post-Gazette reported the incident as an accidental shooting and suicide. It looked no farther for the sources of this episode: alcohol abuse on the IUP campus (not to mention other college campuses), a violent society, the stockpiling of weapons by any number of "ordinary" people in any number of "safe" places, a general belief that words will not do when we have been wronged.

One more story—a brief one—on the flip side. Michael's students are mostly from urban, city neighborhoods in the Bronx, Brooklyn, Manhattan, Queens, and Staten Island. One student, Diane, lives in one of the most notorious housing projects in the Bronx, a place where there aren't just daily shootings and other violent crimes, there are regular arsons, kidnappings, and, as Diane has described, literally dozens of small children, five to ten years old, who spend their entire days outdoors, wandering around unsupervised, not in school, hanging out with crack dealers, prostitutes, and gunrunners. What is incredible is that, after her day of classes at John Jay College, Diane goes home and spends her evenings tutoring the kids in the project. She is teaching them how to read and write because, as she says, "They know the public school is a dangerous place, and they're not going to go." Why does she do this three nights a week from 5:30 to 7:30 p.m.? Because, she says, she is "sick of watching us all die or get sick or be totally lost in society." This young woman is eighteen years old, lives with her sisters and mother, and is a fine student in her own right. She is working for peace as hard as anyone we know.

In the face of such occurrences, we believe that we have no choice but to "dwell" in the problems, and, where possible, in the small triumphs; that is, to work with students to begin, at the very least, to recognize the complexity of the problems and some possible solutions, and to treat them—the students and the issues—seriously, respectfully, and with the kind of depth they deserve.

We try to make peace with the upheavals of the political world, the social environment, the ecology. Or we resist even the idea of making

peace with forces that, if they are not challenged and chang
lives. The classroom is one important place to go to get ͠
been done to us—and what we have done to others. It is the p͠
we can do work that adds needed things to our lives. Or at least it is ͠
place where we can examine all of the above as a community of thinkers
and writers.

In her book, *The Peaceable Classroom*, Mary Rose O'Reilley recalls hearing a question over twenty years ago that has preoccupied her ever since:
"Is it possible to teach English so that people stop killing each other?"
(9). It is difficult for us to hear this question without at once perceiving
its innocence and its desperation. As a species, human beings seem determined to self-destruct. We have exploited resources to the point of
exhausting them. The West celebrates the expansion of our special brand
of economics into the far reaches of the world, ignoring the obvious con-
sequence that these resources will now disappear even more rapidly
under such systems of marketing and consumption. Cynicism thrives
among loosely formed communities whose basis for connection is tensely
balanced fears of sudden death by violence and monstrous neglect by
the rest of society. We read within the pages of countless magazines and
periodicals the same heart-stopping, mind-numbing news that sells the
major newspapers: more and more women will be sexually assaulted
by the time they are in their early twenties; in the new millennium, the
world's population will increase so rapidly that our planet's ability to
support all its occupants could be in question (McKibben 32–35); we
click on our morning news to learn that young children are committing
increasingly violent crimes against both adults and other children; we
learn that the odds for any of us to become victims of violent crime are
continually on the rise; extremists protest against a federal government
by blowing up a government building and hundreds of innocent human beings; someone bombs a passenger jet; someone bombs people
enjoying music at the Olympics; social scientists speculate on television's
influential role in such extremism as statisticians accumulate data about
how many hours of television average Americans will have watched by
age sixty-five—how many murders and assaults we will have "wit-
nessed," how much despair we will have absorbed from news stories,
movies, melodramas, commercials, and a variety of "specials"; every
day in cities throughout the nation, cops go into public elementary and
secondary schools and confiscate guns—sometimes discovering assault
weapons in the hands and lockers of children not old enough to be allowed on amusement park rides without an adult; we overhear young
college students bragging about their weekend dates including unprotected sex with partners they scarcely know; we get to watch made-for-
TV movies about every alleged commission of a crime by someone made

even more notorious by the news media; and we can expect to see the nooks and crannies of everyday life exposed for our viewing appetites as more and more private citizens set up video-surveillance cameras whose tapes are bought up like potato chips and beer by network and cable stations who then show us who we are when we think no one is watching. We discover that someone is *always* watching. Before long, it no longer matters that anyone is watching because everyone is watching and no one is noticing.

This is not the only way to see things. And it can hardly be what we'd want to suggest is the necessary condition of our lives. But while these things are happening, while whole nations of the Earth suffer famine, war, religious persecution, air, land, and water pollution, the tradition of sending children to school to get educated prevails. And so, as always, educators gather to wonder what we are to do, how we are to contribute to well-being, to peace, to human competence in at least the basics of tolerance, community, and the care of our planet and our children.

In striving to understand our students and the ways we educate and the ways our students learn, we simply cannot ignore the fact that the world is not in good health: economics, job prospects, social relationships are as strained as ever. More and more people are ignorant of events in the world because despite the availability of incredible sources of information, we have no way to process it all.

Even more dramatic is the fact that there may not be much we can do to help make our students safe or to help them keep themselves and their loved ones well and safe. While education may reach its hands into the lives of students, those same students are designing their futures fast and furiously, and to a great extent we may be outside of their designs—however much we may or may not like it. Philip Abbot notes, "[t]he fact that we can even imagine what a world composed only of penitentiaries and factories would be like indicates a possible future" (169).

It may be even darker than this. Mary Rose O'Reilley writes,

> As we try to center and recompose ourselves and our students, I think we teachers are in a race with death for the future of human kind. On the one hand, we are learning that all of us are knit together in a web of connections. We are seeing that community-building, group problem solving, and the fostering of mutual interdependence are central to our task as liberal arts teachers and vital to a positive vision of the future. At the same time, lethal forces are on the loose. (138)

What *about* education? What of *other* possible futures? We don't live in our classrooms, yet we are alive in them. We spend hours upon hours in them, planning for them, redesigning the spaces and times in which we will use them. Are we spending this time well? Are *we* well—healthy—while we are spending this time?

Mark:

Right outside my office window, yesterday, a big fight—knife and all. The steel grating across the glass obscured very little of this "exchange." It was a woman, maybe 17 or 18 years old, and another older woman, maybe in her 30s. The younger woman had the knife and kept saying, "You don't fuck with me no more you muthafucka, you keep your ass away from me!" I couldn't hear anything the other woman was saying. The younger one was waving the knife in a wide arc in front of her, and the older woman was evidently trying to smooth-talk her. She obviously wasn't going to turn her back on the knife. There were people gathering and yelling and hooting. I made a quick call to the cops—though I knew they'd be nearby anyway (we are, after all, the College of Criminal Justice). Moments later, a cop showed up and then another. Soon, there were half a dozen cops. I was sitting at my desk, trying to read a thesis proposal on Emile Zola, but having a hard time, as you might imagine. As I watched the scene outside, the young woman spotted me watching. She kicked at the window grating (recall that my office is slightly below street level) and screamed something I couldn't understand; her face was so full of rage, I actually felt shocked. Then, the cops hauled both of them away.

Of course, this stuff happens all the time in New York City—I guess in any city. But the face of that young woman has stayed with me, her anger, her absolute disgust with the intrusion of my attention.

Michael

There is more violence—and more kinds of it—out there than almost any of us are able to comprehend. What should we say about the violence? Is it relevant to our work as composition teachers? Is that a rhetorical question?

We say no; it's a question worth asking and trying to answer. What is the relevance, the role of violence in the work of teaching? No, we are not advocating innovations in corporal punishment! But our students have taught us many things about the kinds of violence that have, to varying extents, framed their lives. They have prompted us to examine our own lives, and we find that violence has been a factor for each of us as well. As composition teachers, we cannot pretend that violence is irrelevant to the work and lives of our students, just as we cannot and would not pretend it is irrelevant to our own lives and work. In trying to find ways to allow for examinations of violence as a significant part of the common knowledge, the danger for teachers is that we are probably not prepared for what arises from such considerations.

And what arises? Questions. Our students wonder what's being done to keep them safe. They wonder how much safety is even possible. They ask what they can do, what we are doing, what they should pay attention to, and if there is something to work toward in the future. We need to say something to them. To tell them new things are coming and that we will work together to be able to understand what they are. They are telling us that they already know things. Or we are telling them that we already know things, or we are forgetting something. We will have to write it down. *Write it down*. Things are happening, and we cannot write them down fast enough or well enough. Everyone is writing something down, and we had better figure out what it is supposed to mean.

———————————

Mark:

Tonight, I'm thinking about how important our teachers have been to us. I'm thinking this, because I'm reading Don [Byrd's] *The Poetics of the Common Knowledge*. I'm thinking about how important Don has been to us both and about how much I am moved by his book. He writes, "I am interested in beings who cause themselves, define themselves, and enclose themselves in their radical uniqueness. I am interested in how they may be understood as acting not from their theories—that is, generalities about their possible formal condition—but from their singularities." This is the provocation we have always sought from Don. ". . . acts of living . . . are insistently and beautifully singular" (2).

I think we are writing *Letters for the Living* because we genuinely appreciate the singularity of every one of our students—or at least we try to. This, I think, has been the sustaining fact of what we do and who we are as teachers, friends, fathers, partners to our partners.

Michael

———————————

Michael:

Your posting reminds me of one of our conversations about "utopia"—and about the need to dream toward a life—a community of lives—that can sustain (and enjoy) a healthy culture. More and more I want to make this book a real link between everyday life and the work of teaching, especially teaching writing. With *Composition and Resistance*, we were trying to make a book that would be evidence of the work of composing among a group of writing teachers who are also writers. I want *Letters for the Living* to be an example of how an ongoing dialogue about our work as writing teachers has also always been a dialogue about the composition(s) of our lives—even if those lives have been laced with trials and tribulations. Especially if there have been trials and tribulations! Proust said, "It is our moments of suffering that outline our books and the intervals of respite that write them" (1022). Maybe we've forgotten about the idea of "respite," but we damn sure have been outlining our work with our griefs!!

Mark

One reason we love working in composition is that we have learned—or been taught—to understand the term "composition" as broadly and imaginatively as possible. Composing is a living process, and it is the living qualities of composition that we value most—the lives of the composers.

Gertrude Stein wrote,

> The composition is the thing seen by every one living in the living they are doing, they are the composing of the composition that at the time they are living is the composition of the time in which they are living. It is that that makes living a thing they are doing. Nothing else is different, of that almost anyone can be certain. . . . (516)

We compose and we are the composing. Then why haven't teachers across the profession used the word "composition" in more "living" ways? Why do some of us decide in advance of the composition class, before Monday morning, before any single student's composing, which compositions are permissible and which are not; which are possible and which are not? Why do some of us limit the forms of the living at this time in human history?

In *Letters for the Living*, we choose to invoke the word "composing" as comprehensively as we can: to make, craft, build, write, organize, soothe, comfort, pull together. Students in our composition classes can meaningfully make essays and demonstrate academically acceptable prose, but they can as meaningfully make fictions, poetry, and talk. James Berlin suggested we can act from a confluence of poetics and rhetoric. We can recognize the social function—and functioning—of the imagination. We can observe the collapsing of the personal and social realms of our compositions as we make visions and plans for better ways of living, as we look and work for political inspiration. "Let's all be poets," Mary Rose O'Reilley writes. "Let's make this so much a part of our self-definition that nobody stands out, nobody has to be asked, 'who do you think you are?'" (89). And we can make our classrooms the places where, following the lead of Geneva Smitherman's writings, languages meet and people talk; places where people create the unique, places where people, in their uniqueness, may work together to examine differences and to explore common ground. As poet Vicente Huidobro writes,

> Es preciso crear la luz y el sueño
> En el hueco de la mano
> (We have to create light and dreams
> In the palm of the hand) (202/203)

But we are almost out of time—class is almost over, the curriculum spent, the year ended, the country bankrupt, the culture spoiled, the world ruined. Most of the students we teach face abuse every day—as we write—as you read: but they are not dead yet—and neither are we. There is light and there are dreams still to be realized.

Twenty years ago, Molefi Kete Asante called for an "aggressive beginning," for using the power in our heads, hearts, and hands, our compositions: "Language is the instrument of conveyance of attitudes and perceptions, and these symbols must play havoc with symbolic structure" (56). Havoc to disrupt the ways in which people with power hurt people without power: it's that simple and that complex. And it's getting that late.

To: Our children: Daina and Cory Blitz and Roland Hurlbert
Re: Dreams

Dear Daina, Cory, and Roland:

It feels strange and exhilarating to write an e-mail letter into the future. That's what this is. Not much different from the traditional, mysterious envelope that appears at the reading of a will. The heirs open the letter with shaky hands to read what the dearly departed has left them in words composed by the living hands now folded in repose. Well, this is less melodramatic. Of course you don't have e-mail accounts (yet!), but composing this in the medium of programmable light, imprinting it onto a chip that will bear this ghostly message for as long as such chips are readable—that's one of the strange parts. You'll find this one day—not as an electronic message, but as a printed page in a book whose raw materials are friendship, a pair of teaching and writing careers, the lives we have lived, and many thousands of electronic letters your fathers have exchanged over the years.

Writing into the future. And teaching for a future. Maybe these seem like the phrases of people who are nearing a milestone of years. At the moment, your dads are still looking forward to many years of doing what we do, of enjoying our children and watching you make your tracks. But between the two of us, we've also logged nearly forty years of teaching—junior high to doctoral students. We must have learned something.

In so many ways, you, our children, have been our measures. What we do, we do with you in mind. When we have conversations with students and listen to stories about their dreams for a life beyond their current circumstances, we have had a sense that we are also listening to a conversation we will be having with our own kids. At this writing, the sum total of your ages is about 19 (Daina, you are now 9; Cory, you're 6; and Roland, you're 7), around the age of our typical college students. When we think about the utopian ideas that pass through our hands and before our eyes as we work in higher education, we know we are participants in a mystery. What will it take to do something tangible, something real that will make their paths even slightly more clear to our students? What will it take for us to do the same for you?

We have a lot of questions for you. Were we right to spend so many hours grinding through thousands of pages of writing by people we would know only for a few years—all the while not spending those hours listening to you, laughing with you, reading with you? Were the hours we spent with you the best hours we had in us? Had we spent ourselves in academic work that, too, often, felt terribly distant from actual teaching and learning? We know you watched us work our way through reports and committee work; we felt your eyes waiting for the "little bit later" when we'd take a break from editing an article or writing commentary on someone's thesis. Did it seem strange to you that other adults would say they were envious of teachers for all our free time even as you wondered why we seemed to have almost none?

What should we do in a world that's come undone? What stories must we teach you? What stories will you tell? What reasonable hope do we have that you will survive to tell stories? What world(s) do our teachings reflect? Are any of these the right questions? We're still asking.

With all our love,

Your Dads

Notes

1. The symposium, Problems of Affirmation in Cultural Theory (P.A.C.T.), was sponsored by the Society for Critical Exchange and was held at Case Western Reserve University, Cleveland, Ohio, in October 1991. The other participants were David Downing, James Sosnoski, Nancy Mack, Richard Ohman, Evan Watkins, Elspeth Stuckey, Victor Vitanza, Steven Mailloux, Barbara Beisecker, Brian Caraher, Jeanne Colleran, Mary Jean Corbett, James Creech, Laura Donaldson, Philip Goldstein, Patricia Harkin, Lila Hanft, Brett Harwood, Ann

Lowry, Brian Macaskill, Laura Maruca, Patrick McHugh, Robert Miklitsch, Patrick Murphy, Takis Poulakis, James Phelan, Bonnie Shaker, Gary Lee Stonum, Jennifer Waters, and Martha Woodmansee.

2. Throughout *Letters for the Living* we have included excerpts from our e-mail to each other. For the sake of clarity and economy, and for matters of style, we have edited the postings where necessary, and we have trimmed the mastheads and closings to include only our first names.

3. Since the posting of this e-mail, the Federal Minimum Wage has been increased by 90 cents per hour. Employers may continue to pay teenagers less during a "probationary" period.

4. All students' writings are quoted or paraphrased with their written permission. We have gone to extraordinary lengths to protect our students' identities. *None of the names we use for any student in this book is the real one.* We have also edited the personal facts we report about our students' lives in order to further ensure their privacy. Finally, we have edited grammar and spelling as little as possible in our students' writing in an attempt to respect and present individual voices.

5. We argue, after Fu, that composing can help us become less strange to ourselves and to others. In the poetics of the Russian Formalist Victor Shklovsky, "making strange" (*ostranenie*) is a way of discovering the everyday, of making it available to critical inquiry. Terence Hawkes writes,

> According to Shklovsky, the essential function of poetic art is to counteract the process of habituation encouraged by routine everyday modes of perception. The aim of poetry is to *defamiliarize* that with which we are overly familiar, to 'creatively deform' the usual, the normal, and so to inculcate a new, childlike, non-jaded vision in us. The poet thus aims to disrupt 'stock responses', and to generate heightened awareness: to restructure our ordinary perception of 'reality', so that we end by *seeing* the world instead of numbly recognizing it: or at least so that we end by designing a 'new' reality to replace the (no less fictional) one which we have inherited and become accustomed to (62).

So, while we make the concept of "becoming less strange to ourselves" an important part of our theorizing in this book, we also recognize the possibilities of the inverse properties of strangeness.

Introduction to Part 2

Michael:

At the NCTE Annual Convention in Pittsburgh, at the Meade Award panel, I talked about *Social Issues in the English Classroom*. Something I was asked haunts me: "What did you leave out of the book? Is there an issue that you wished the book addressed that it doesn't?"

I said, "Yes, violence."

Mark

2 Violence

It sometimes seems to us that there are as many maps of the field of composition as there are people writing about composition. Whether by James Berlin, Stephen North, C. H. Knoblauch, Lester Faigley, Harriet Malinowitz, or Sherrie Gradin, each of these maps offers interesting or alternative versions of the rhetorics with which we work.

The discipline of rhetoric and composition teaches how to value personal writing, forms of exposition and argument, and how to regard our students' writings as linguistic, rhetorical, and cultural events. The maps of composition offer meaningful certainty as we name the kind of teachers of composition we want to be. They give us confidence as we construct our pedagogies for the imagined subjectivities we hope to affect and the agency we hope to inspire.

But what happens when we find ourselves in a classroom experience which not only demands that we have paid attention to what we have learned from those who chart the profession, but which calls on us to improvise? Sometimes, with little or no prompting, students recreate disturbing acts of violence in their writings. Our received rhetorical, theoretical, and pedagogical knowledge does not, alone, prepare us for these discourses which, to be honest, baffle, disorient, or leave us searching in a state where decisive language and action are suspended. But the fact is that sometimes when we are in the classroom, the only map of rhetoric and pedagogy that we can make is an anecdotal map in which we collect the various stories told to us by our students, a collection we share with our friends and colleagues with the idea of creating a deep history of shared experiences. This history offers a chance for generating deep understandings of what we do, which, in turn, supplies us with opportunities for becoming more prepared for our work as teachers—and as makers of maps. *Letters for the Living*, then, is one attempt to peel away some theoretical abstractions so that we might better understand the personal and cultural implications of what each student is telling us, the uniqueness of each student, of each life. No one encounters violence or peace in general. The experience of each is always unique.

In making *Letters for the Living*, we drew a good deal of inspiration from a particular few teachers—some we know well and personally, some we know "only" through their books, their talks, their visible effects on the lives of their students and their colleagues. One such writer is Mary Rose O'Reilley, whose book *The Peaceable Classroom* offers an absolutely living perspective on what can and must be done in classrooms and schools if we are to provide an education that has anything to do with peace and freedom. Perhaps some readers will see that aim as too lofty, or even unrelated to the business of teaching composition. We would disagree. Encouraged by O'Reilley's courageous book, we are arguing that to ignore violence as a reality in the lives of our students and ourselves, to see peace and freedom as irrelevant goals of education, is to invite a living death into our classrooms, to encourage an insensitivity to living in the culture and a numbness to death.

Mary Rose O'Reilley writes:

> Most academic brutalization is more subtle than the cases of corporal punishment most of us have come across from time to time. . . . By being insulted, bullied, and turned into objects, young people learn to insult, bully, and turn others into objects. These actions contain the seeds of violence. It follows, therefore, that the first step in teaching peace is to examine the ways in which we are already teaching conflict.
>
> It works. Punishment works. Violence works, at least in the short term. I guess that's why we keep doing it. It's easy, too, and takes little thought. "It's the only thing they understand." . . .
>
> Violence is easy. Nonviolence, by contrast, takes all we have and costs not less than everything. (31)

Nonviolence costs everything, and violence costs everything. How spent a culture are we?

We need a vision of what is possible, and we must also face what is before us in our everyday line of sight. Our students bring incredibly complicated lives to our classrooms. So do teachers. Students bring their trials and successes, their desperation, their fatigue, their boredom, their excitement, their expectations for a change in the way things are. And so do teachers. Our students offer us, at every turn, a resiliency in a culture that may not, for them, offer much hope of a vision beyond television or state-sponsored lotteries. And we offer—or our role as educators promises—alternatives. Or do we? Where can we begin?

One place might be in ideas of community. We have attempted, as often as possible, to involve our students in projects that entail community effort among participants. In some cases, these collaborations (small and large) must find ways of connecting with other communities within and outside the classroom. The point for us, here, is to work toward an environment in which participants are designing and constructing things—in writing and in other kinds of actions—which can point up alternatives to a world in which everything feels used up or hopeless or unhealthy.

When composition teachers listen, they hear things. When we read, we find things. What do we do with what we hear and find? Do we turn a deaf ear? Do we look the other way or look only at sentences and paragraphs and style and form? Do we remind students of the end-of-term writing exam? Do we tell them how sorry we are when we hear that they have been victimized in any one of a hundred ways, but that they and we have other obligations? Do we remind ourselves how difficult it is to deal with their problems and so find a way to get them to keep their problems to themselves?

What kind of madness is this? You may be outraged to think anybody would treat students in this way, but we all know teachers and others that do. Composition teachers have figured out ways to make just about any form of writing relevant in the composition classroom, but what happens when some of that writing takes up issues, questions, confessions and confusions for which few composition teachers are prepared? What can we do when we discover that a pedagogy of expository writing means people are going to expose things about their lives—and about ours, as well? Haven't teachers throughout the humanities taught, all through the years, that good writing touches people, that it hits nerves and moves people? What happens when our students touch us, hit our nerves, move us with writings and conversations about themselves, whether or not they contain a capital "I"? These are not questions for which we find easy answers, but they are the questions for which we *must* have answers.

Michael:

It's the third day of the semester. I just met with my Composition class for the second time. Today we discussed the major class assignment for the first half of the semester, their individually written books (the first day of class, after going over the syllabus and having the students introduce themselves to each other, I asked them to examine and discuss a sample of books from last semester's students and come prepared today to talk about, however tentatively, book projects they might take on.)*

Today, as the class sat in a circle, reporting on their ideas, one student said she wanted to write her book about the physical abuse of women by their boyfriends. She had looked at the kinds of personal issues raised in some of

---

*We discuss our book assignments in detail in Part 5.

last semester's books and was clearly moved. She said her boyfriend had beaten her up so badly she had had to be hospitalized. He was arrested and spent time in jail. She said she wanted to write this book for other women because, as she put it, no one should have to suffer what she had. I noticed that many of the women in the class were nodding their heads.

I told the student that she could, if she wanted, change her topic at a later date if she found that writing it or sharing it with the class proved to be too painful for her. I also told her that, in the interest of discretion, she should probably change the names, time, and setting of the attacks. I even suggested that she might choose to publish the book anonymously.

After class this student said she would not change her mind about writing this book and that, yes, she would protect the identities of everyone in it and that she might even choose anonymous publication. Michael, as she spoke to me I noticed her growing more and more shaky. Her face was getting redder, and before long she had tears in her eyes. She told me that she would more than likely be missing some classes at some point in the semester as she still had to go to the hospital to have "another operation." She also said she would bring a doctor's excuse.

Mark

Mark:

One of John Jay's students was shot and killed when she ran toward the gunshots that killed her boyfriend. He had just been shot by a couple of dealers who then saw her and wanted no witnesses.

Michael

Michael:

A student came to my office yesterday. She had, for her first paper, which could have been on any topic of her choice, written about how a boyfriend used to beat her up, about how he once drove her into the country, stopped the car and dragged her into the woods and beat her—how she fell and went into a fetal position and how he kept kicking her until she stopped crying— picked her up—took her back to his car and started to treat her with "affec- tion." Yesterday, she brought a poem to my office. It was about suicide. I told her I didn't think I could just respond to the poem without acknowledging that it seemed like more than a poem. We talked about counseling, to help her with what she called her "confusion."

Today she stayed after class to tell me she would be out of class next time because she has an "appointment."

Mark

———————————

Michael:

Such a strange morning.

I went to the Squirrel Hill Barnes & Noble here in Pittsburgh. As I roamed around, I suddenly had a mental image of one of my undergraduate classes. They were sitting there, looking early morning and innocent in their Indiana University of Pennsylvania sweatshirts. They were staring at me as if class were about to start. They did not seem to notice that there was blood smeared all over them and all over the walls and all over their faces and IUP sweatshirts.

I feel like there were words smeared in blood across the back wall of my classroom, but I couldn't make them out and yet I must make them out if I am going to stop the bleeding. I feel like I've got a screw loose for having waking images like this and for walking the streets of Squirrel Hill afterwards, shocked and sweating. I wonder where I get off trying to save the world.

Mark

———————————

Mark:

It sounds like you had a vision, my friend. There may be blood on and in every wall, everywhere we look (and more where we fail to look).

Michael

———————————

Michael:

I hope that *Letters for the Living* can be read as a serious attempt to tell a fuller story of what happens, of what it means to live and teach composition in these times. We teach in a culture thick with pain—and also joy and love. And no one has adequately chronicled the day to day of our professional lives. There's so much that the profession needs to talk about and prepare ourselves for, to address and redress—and even admit—and so little of it gets taken up. Worse, it probably wouldn't make sense if it did. How can there be so much talk about "professional issues" such as "evaluation" and "authority" and, yes, even "grammar," and so much silence about how our jobs connect to the real living we do? Not to mention real grieving.

The profession is pressed by concerns that sometimes don't concern me or you, I know. I am thinking of the young woman who was killed after witnessing her boyfriend's murder. What does your student's death mean to your students? to you? to your colleagues? to your teaching? to our profession? How does our teaching acknowledge the cruelty of this event and other examples of outrageousness in our students' lives? How does our living and teaching respond to this death?

Mark

———————————

Mark:

You would be amazed by the number of times my students have reported in class that they saw a shooting or beating somewhere in New York on their way to class. That they negotiate their ways through real and all-too-physical dangers is a testament to the fact that they place real hope in what they do at the college. Sometimes I believe their hope is unfounded. Can I do enough for them? Can I do the right things for them?

I know we try hard to figure out what we're doing, but as we examine academic life and our various roles in it, too often I feel like I don't know what the hell I'm doing. Why are there so many books and articles whose authors seem to know exactly what to do in any given situation, in any given classroom? I don't know how to use so many of those things any more. Maybe worse, I don't believe most of it—I don't trust where it's coming from.

I do know we could hurt someone. Our students could hurt someone. Maybe we are hurting someone.

Michael

———————————

Michael:

It would be the height of arrogance for us to say that what we do doesn't matter or effects no change.

Something important sometimes happens in our classes, and I suspect that we have very little to do with it—except that we've got the brains to get out of the way.

Mark

———————————

Mark:

Last semester, in my English 101 class, my students spent the last 5 weeks of the course writing small books on topics they considered inherently "important." I wasn't much more directive in making the assignment than that. They had to try to find both primary and secondary source material and/or to include visuals and some kind of annotated bibliography. Some students chose to write about things the popular press say are important: "abortion," "homelessness," "drug-abuse" and so on. But a few students wrote about very personal matters, struggling to make the personally profound into something a public would accept as *also* inherently important. One woman, Celia, wrote about how painful it has been to visit her boyfriend in prison on Riker's Island. He's in his early 20s; she is 19. She gets harassed, grabbed, verbally abused by other inmates and by corrections officers. "Once you walk through the first gate and it closes. Your in their hands now." She wrote of having to learn how to listen to her boyfriend's complaints, his fears—particularly disillusioning to her because she and her boyfriend have both always been really strong city kids. At Riker's, she wrote, "He's just a little man who has to worry about being raped or beat up. One of the [gang members] wouldn't even let him use the phone when it was his turn."

Another student, Gina, wrote about her disillusionment with being the girlfriend of a member of the [gang]. For a while, at age 17, she was being driven around in a big Mercedes, was *given* a BMW to drive around town in. She didn't have a license, but she was tooling around Manhattan and the Bronx in her Beemer. She said she was also privy to shootings, torture, robbery, ritual "sexing in" of female members, and so on. When other female gang members began pressuring her to join, she broke up with her boyfriend. A friend of hers did join and was "sexed in" by having to have oral sex with ten men and then "screw" her "choice" of five of them—all in one night—all unprotected.

Mark, this is a level of violence most people can scarcely believe when they read about it in the newspaper or watch an evening news profile of gang life. But it's going on right here. The young people we teach experience violence as a "normal" feature of their social whole—it's just life on the street. "Harm is valued because it produces justice" and then "retributive justice" (Felson and Tedeschi 155). But our students also know that this violent "justice" is destroying their lives and their society, and when my students speak up about it, they do so knowing that they are living a life with a bullet aimed right at them.

Michael

Michael:

Let me tell you about a book I received last semester. It was written by Frank, who came to IUP from a small town in east-central Pennsylvania. Frank relates how he and a group of neighborhood children became inseparable friends. Friends, that is, until one of them, "Greg", began to act strangely. (I should add that Frank knows Greg well enough to know how he thinks. In addition, Frank procured permission from the appropriate people to tell this story.) At first, Greg became more and more of a loner. Then he broke into the house of one of the group, Jon. He stole Jon's mother's credit cards and segmented the family's goldfish with a knife. After the friends all decided that Greg was the guilty party, they shunned him.

The climax of Frank's book, which I am about to quote at length, is about how Greg took revenge on Jon's family, for the shunning.

> All he had to do was wait. "I hate them," he thought, and then smiled when he thought of what he would soon be doing to them. Greg looked at his watch. 10:23 PM. It was time. He took the rubber surgical gloves out of his pocket and put them on. "No fingerprints," he said chuckling. He crept around to the back and put his hand on the door knob. The latch made a small click, as the handle turned. "It was open, I knew it would be," Greg thought. . . He knew exactly where to walk since he'd been in the house a hundred times. He always came this way. He opened the door to the kitchen and it creaked, "Shhh," and walked in. It was dark in there, perfect. He listened. Nothing. Greg took off his pants and shoes and left them by the door. "I'll get them on the way out," he thought. He walked toward the stairs in his underwear, stopped for a second and realized how funny he looked. He wasn't wearing any shoes or pants, he had on surgical gloves and was carrying a knife. He laughed softly to himself and continued toward the steps. He knew what steps to skip over to avoid the creaking. He was upstairs now. Jon's door was closed. Greg knew that Jon was a heavy sleeper and probably wouldn't hear the screams of his sisters being raped. Their door was open. He thought about the bitch, he hated her. She wouldn't let him swim there after the fish incident. They never proved anything and they still blamed him. He hated them for that. "I should have killed the fucking cats too," he thought. "I'll have my revenge tonight," Greg whispered and tiptoed past Brenda's room into the girl's room. They look so pretty sleeping. His heart started beating faster. Greg walked over to the bed and put his hand on Heather's back. She was fast asleep.
>   "What are you doing in here Greg," Sue [the other sister woke up and saw him] said. She saw the knife and started to scream, "Mom!!!!"
>   "Shut up bitch," Greg started to move towards her. The door flew open and Brenda came in.
>   "Greg, is that you, what the hell are you doing," Brenda [the mother] said. "Get out of my house. Heather go get Jon up."
>   Greg turned toward her and she saw the knife.
>   "Run," she screamed to her daughters.
>   He started to slash, it felt so good, he hated that bitch. She tried to protect herself but it was no use. The blade cut her hands, her face. She fell, Greg chuckled. He knew he would love this moment. Then he remembered Jon. The girls went to wake him up. Jon was stronger than him. Greg left Brenda on the floor to die and walked over to Jon's room. Heather was in there trying to wake him up. She saw Greg and the blood, she screamed and ran. Greg walked over to Jon's bed. The idiot was still asleep. Greg raised the knife and slashed Jon's neck. "Good night," he said. Greg knew that he had to catch the girls, they'd tell. He ran down stairs and out the front door. They were already half way down the block screaming. Greg was scared, He ran. He dropped the knife

and ran home. He got to his house and realized he forgot his shoes and pants. They'd be coming for him soon. He wanted to panic. His Mom was awake and saw he was covered in blood. She knew she had to act fast to save her son. "get in the shower," she said. "Give me your clothes," they were drenched in blood.

The girls made it to a neighbor's house and called the police, for once they came fast.

Frank then tells how the girls identified Greg and how the police went to Greg's house and arrested him as his mother tried in vain to protect her son. After that:

Greg was charged with two counts of attempted murder and a list of other things. He was charged as an adult. His bail was set at two hundred and fifty thousand dollars and a hearing date was set. Greg would be in an adult jail with adult men. He would pay for his crimes in more ways than he knew.

A search of Greg's house revealed no additional clues to the crime. Several sets of house keys, including ours, and some stolen credit cards were recovered. No bloody shirt or underwear. The police didn't worry. They had this kid. They had three witnesses, his pants and shoes, the knife, . . . They chuckled when they thought about a fifteen year old boy in the state prison. "Those big guys in there will take care of him in there," I heard one cop say, "I'll bet they will line up just to take turns baby-sitting him." This kid deserved what he got.

Time would heal the Birds' wounds, both physically and mentally. They would be all right. Me, Jon, Jess, and Braden all got together and talked about what had happened. We always knew that he had problems but none of us ever expected this. It was crazy. We all went our separate ways. I left for college, they are all still in high school, and Greg, just weird to think that someone who came to your birthday parties, slept over at your house, and you called a friend, would ever do something like that. It makes me wonder if those nights when my dog would start wildly barking at the night, if Greg was outside, lurking in the bushes.

I know what Frank was burning to tell the world: that none of us is truly safe. Michael, my students mostly come from rural and small towns, but their work suggests that they justifiably do not always feel safe. I don't mean that we should suggest in *Letters for the Living* that living is, at the end of this millennium, impossible for everyone. This is no television show.

Another student who, like Frank, is from a small Pennsylvania town, wrote her book about a high school friend whom she calls Lynne. Lynne went to Ocean City, Maryland, the summer after her high school graduation for a vacation with some of their girlfriends. While there, Lynne was picked up by a guy in a nightclub. He raped and murdered her. Near the end of the book, the author writes:

Lynne never expected to live until she was old. In fact, she never planned to live to go to college or have a career. When people would ask her what she wanted to do, when she was out of school, she would answer them by saying that she didn't plan to be alive that long. Lynne didn't plan to be alive, in order to have a career at the end of high school. Somehow she knew that she was not going to be around.

Mark

———————————

Mark:

Matthew was a student in one of my composition classes. He sat in the back of the room with his buddy. They would snicker throughout class for the first couple of weeks, making cynical remarks about the project proposals of their classmates, choosing the paths of least resistance in their own writings, and spending, at most, 10 minutes per short assignment. I've got to be truthful; these two irritated the crap out of me, especially Matthew.

One day I asked Matthew if I could speak with him after class about his proposal to write a how-to book for opening a bottle of beer. I also said I'd like to talk to him about something else, and that perhaps his friend should wait outside the room. Matthew said, "I don't care. He can hear—whatever." It occurred to me to let them both know, at the same time, how irritating their behavior was in the class, and I told them so. As I recall, I said something like, "Are you guys aware that after nearly everything anyone in the room says, one or both of you start giggling and talking audibly, distracting the rest of us and showing your colleagues real disrespect?" All I remember is that Matthew said, "Really?" and his pal said, "Other people do it, too." Matthew said, "Are you saying that this is going to affect our grades?" I said, "It is very likely it will, yes." Matthew said, "OK, then, we'll stop."

Anyway, Matthew put off doing his book until only a few days before it was due. He came to me to say he realized he had been wasting his time and mine, and that if I would read it seriously, without prejudice, he'd like to try to write a book on an "actual topic," as he put it. I told to him to go ahead.

His book was less than half the required 10-page length and contained only writing (which is allowed, but most students include some sort of graphics, photos, appendixes, lyrics, something extra). It was entitled, *A Light at the End of a Long Dark Tunnel: A View of Society Through a Young Professional.* I was thinking that the title promised far more than a few pages could deliver. Perhaps I was wrong.

Again, bear in mind that the assignment was, like so many of your own, to write a booklet about something the student considers "important" for his or her readers to know about. In his introduction, Matthew writes:

> I am eighteen years old and have seen things in my life most adults will never see, with the exception of TV. I began volunteering for an ambulance corps when I was fourteen years old. . .

These stories are a recollection of how I have seen some of the worst of society. However, I can not say I wasn't one of them.

Matthew goes on to tell about a few emergency cases he handled. Toward the end of the book, he writes this account:

During my short non-paid career, I've seen some pretty violent scenes. None were as bad as one [particular] night. It had been a quiet Saturday night and my regular crew chief and driver bailed out to go partying. Fortunately the two best looking women in my corps weren't doing anything so they filled in. At around eleven o'clock that night we were about to log off with the city EMS when they called us. (It is very common for city EMS to call volunteers for extra calls that are back-logged). It was a call for a rape victim at the [Motel] on [the Blvd.] near [the] Airport. En route we were given the room number and when we arrived we discovered we were the only medical crew. There were a lot of cops there. Nothing could have prepared me for what happened next. My partners, [B] and [L], went in first, the last thing a rape victim wants to see is a man. [B] immediately started talking to the young woman sitting on the bed crying. There was blood all over the bed and floor leading to the bathroom. When a cop finally spoke all she could say was,

"She's not the victim."

[B] asked where she was and the cop pointed to the bathroom. Because of all the blood leading to it, I jumped over a chair to the bathroom door. When I looked inside it looked like something out of a Freddie Kruger movie. There was blood on everything. In the bathtub was the victim lying in about two inches of bloody water. She had tear wounds around her genitals and bruises on her arms, face and chest. She was [a toddler].

The [young] mother was arrested for permitting her [older] boy friend to rape her daughter. The man could not be found.

Later that night a police car rolled up on our ambulance and asked us to come down to the station house. When we got there two Hospital ambulances were already there. As I walked in I saw my friend [V] and his partner and behind them sitting at the desk were two good friends of mine, [D] and [R], both excellent Paramedics. [B] and [L] talked to [D] and [R] while I went up to [V].

"What's up?" I asked.

"They got him." [V] said smiling.

What happened next was a once in a lifetime ordeal. In the holding room a.k.a. "the cage" was this guy all by himself. The cop opened the cell and walked out of the room. The guy was handcuffed to the cell bench but he still struggled to make an escape. First [D] and [R] went in. All I heard was the man scream like a baby twice then the sound of someone spitting. [V]'s partner leaned over and asked which one was the blackbelt. [V] laughed and answered,

"[D], in two arts."

When the ladies had left the room they both felt the same maybe even more sick. I later found out that they were the ones who had to remove the baby's body. The guy was a mess. As [V] and I left a young cop came in to finish the arrest report to fill in what injuries the perp received while resisting arrest. He was only convicted of rape, not murder, because her dying was an accident.

Mark, a toddler is raped and killed. And Matthew, who simply is at his limit for sensitivity in recounting this story, is the EMT on the scene who must try to make sense of it. I certainly wasn't going to grade his book on the basis of his having lived through a harrowing experience. The book had tremendous shortcomings, and his effort all semester long was less than nil. But the book was his first and only attempt to say something that mattered to him. I guess it was a sort of confession, though he ends the book by citing rape statistics, victim-age statistics, and then calls for greater enforcement of rape laws.

What view of life can someone like Matthew have? I know this was an extraordinary experience, and it was also extraordinary to read about it. I can't help supposing Matthew's had many nightmares about this. On the other hand, he doesn't seem particularly sensitive to his fellow human beings. Once, in a class discussion on ways in which the government, or the Law, is connected to everyday experience, a student spoke about being worried about the possibility of laws that would restrict or forbid abortions. She explained that her sister had had an abortion as soon as she discovered she was pregnant, but that as a 17 year old, she might have had to face parental notification, or worse, if the laws change. Matthew's contribution to this discussion was to say something like, "Your sister should've known better."

Michael

Our students know all too well about suffering and death. And whether they are our most likable students or those with whom we may feel little connection, they come to our classrooms with questions about death that demand answers. "Why are we dying in these ways? Who gets to die of old age? Why don't we feel like we can look forward to long lives?" They need to know if these ways of dying that they see around them can be understood. We don't know. How can we know what to teach someone who has seen a brother murdered, a father killed in an industrial accident, a mother waste away from illness, a sister who has disappeared into street life—the street death? What is there to say? They come to us not just to expose and express the personal, but to hear something life-affirming, peace-giving. Can we give them that? Can we teach anyone to give this to themselves? What if we can't?

Mark:

I am discovering, little by little, through a disturbing series of confessional writings, that a number of my female students, particularly those from Jamaica, have been incestuously raped as children. Generally, the father has been the rapist, and so far, I know of 4 women to whom this has happened (out of 36 students, 20 of whom are women). Other women in the class write of abuses they have suffered more recently. One wrote a poem about her years living with a violent man. The poem is about her struggle to leave this man and her subsequent recovery, and it was chosen for an award for Women's History Month.

Yet another of the women in the same class, a quiet, frightened-looking, 24-year-old, writes stories ranging from wistful romance to violence-poisoned relationships. I know that she was with someone for a while who was abusive, drank heavily (as did she, until recently), and who, I believe, died. She says she is bitter about this bit of her history, having loved and hated this man and now not ever being able to reconcile his death or their lives together. To make matters worse, she's living at home again, and she and her father evidently do battle, physically, on a daily basis. She often looks so unhappy. She rarely talks, but she writes eloquently in her journal which she knows I'll read and respond to.

I read, in a piece entitled "Violence by and against Women: A Comparative and Cross National Analysis," that "studies indicate that women in many, if not most, countries are at greater risk of encountering violence in their own homes than on the streets" (Kruttschnitt 95). And "National Crime Victimization Survey (NCVS) data from the United States indicate that women's rates of being seriously assaulted by a relative are twice that of men's" (Reiss & Roth 1993, as cited in Kruttschnitt 94). To top it off, "Younger women [15-24 years old] appear to be at greater risk of non-lethal violent victimizations than older women" (Kruttschnitt 93).

I don't know how some of these young women—and men—continue.

Michael

Michael:

One student I am teaching is an alternative culture type: black hair, likes cool music, wears Chuck Taylors; a returning student—thoughtful—very quiet. When she speaks, brilliance. When I read her portfolio, I find writings that floor me. In one she tells about being in a class at IUP when a girl in an orange sweater sat down next to her. The sweater triggered an image from her past, of her neighbor being taken out of his house in an orange body bag after a heroin overdose. She writes: "For years that death bag would float up from nowhere and hover around me while I tried to eat my cereal, or read, or just about anything I tried to do." She continues: "I still remember how the paramedics carried him out, and plopped him on the ground in an upright position. He sat there on the cold pavement with that orange death bag clinging to him. They weren't fooling me, I knew he was in there and I knew he was dead."

Michael, this student is from yet another small town in central Pennsylvania. The violence and pain is everywhere: towns, cities, in our classrooms, hovering around millions of orange sweaters. As I read her portfolio, I can't help but think about how by telling each other about our students, we are learning about a kind of eloquence in storytelling that, if we're not careful in how we pay attention, almost belies the realities that provoke it.

Another student, a woman in her early twenties who is putting herself through college by working part time in a Pittsburgh steel mill, wrote in her book, *D. O. A.*, about finding her uncle, dead from a heroin overdose, in his apartment:

> I proceed into the kitchen, and there he was! I pretty much ran into him. He was sitting at his kitchen table against the wall. I didn't even think it was him at first. The upper half of his body was slumped to the right side, sort of upside down. He probably would have fallen if it wasn't for the wall. His arms, head, and neck were completely purple. You could see blood on the floor, obviously from the purging. Even as I write this, I can still picture him in front of me. It still doesn't look like him. "You fucking asshole," I said quietly to him. "do you know what this is going to do to everyone? Do you even care?" I looked at the rest of the kitchen. Saw the bag the rest of his shit was in, and felt like shoving it down his throat. "Here uncle Michael, is what you want, well here it is."

Mark

Michael:

Yesterday in my Humanities Literature class, we were reading a piece that dealt with homosexual desire in some pretty explicit ways. I had the students bring their journals, exchange at random with one another, and write their reactions to and ideas about the reading so far. Then they gave the notebooks back and did short readings from them in class.

After class one student came up to me, and he said, "Mark, you better see what someone wrote in my journal—at least the very ending of it." At the end of a long scribbled page, I saw something that went like this: "I'm a Christian. And I've got one thing to say to all of the faggots. It's a good day for Genocide." I told the owner of the journal: "Well this just goes to show how much this person has to learn, but then we all have a lot to learn." I hid it, but I was angry as hell. I thought about it all day and talked it over with a colleague. Here's my plan. On Tuesday, the next time the class meets, I will put the students into groups. I will join the journal owner's group and will have a public reason for seeing the journal. Then I will ask the student who wrote this entry to come to my office and inform him of the existence of hate laws and how perilous his enrollment at IUP could be if he writes threatening things to people. The important thing, I know, is not to lose this guy because he does indeed have so much to learn, but the reality is I'd like to tell him to get out of my class.

OK—so I can't love all of my students, but, as their teacher, I feel they are all in my care.

Mark

Mark:

On an invitation, I went to an area high school today. It's an inner city school sorely lacking in resources, maintenance, and physical space. Clearly there are enormous tensions among students and faculty, between students, and so on. The first class I visited was an 11th grade English class that was studying poetry and urban life.

The students were reading poems by Hughes, Giovanni, and Baraka. They also looked at a lot of poems by my students. They seemed impressed. A few showed me poems they had written. One poem was particularly disturbing. As I recall, it ended something like:

> People kill and one day I will.

Toward the end of the period, a very scarred (knife-line on his face) Black man with a very deep voice asked, "When your class reads poems that show anger at the white man, do you get upset?" I said, "Sometimes I do." He nodded, as if he'd guessed right. I told him that sometimes I feel impressed by the honesty, and sometimes I feel weary because of the truth of it, and sometimes I feel honored because I have been invited to read or to listen to someone's feelings.

He nodded again. It may have been my imagination, but the mood felt different—better—in the room. I was invited back. And I invited the students to sit in on my class(es) when they could. They evidently found this idea astonishing and looked at their teacher. She nodded; they wanted, immediately, to make specific arrangements with me.

The other class I visited was a senior class in Argument Writing. Of the 28 students enrolled, 6 came. The teacher, in his second year, was so embarrassed. I reassured him that a class beginning at 7:50 in the morning was a challenge for anyone. The six who came were quite good and were prepared. They just had absolutely no interest in their own writings. They had been asked to argue for or against a two-party political system because that's what they were discussing in their social studies classes.

And so, I listened to the six papers and made a few comments. I asked them lots of questions about arguing. I asked them how they argued with parents, friends, teachers, brothers and sisters. I asked them how they distinguish between arguing and bickering, arguing and fighting. They seemed to enjoy this discussion. I asked them whether there were any elements of bickering that would serve in a more formal argument (and vice versa). What about fighting? Most agreed that "fighting" generally resulted in violence; a few suggested that even bickering and arguing could be violent.

Anyway, I returned to JJC in the afternoon, feeling *grateful* for my job, proud of my students (more than ever), and in awe of the thousand years you spent teaching high school. The classes I saw today made me wonder how I would do my job with ever fewer resources, with such spotty attendance and with a more prescribed curriculum. Then again, there was a lot of living in that school I visited today.

Michael

———————————————

Michael:

A student from my Basic Writing class—very quiet, a very hard worker—came into my office today with her paper. Her paper told the story of her father's death the previous week.

Her father was a laid-off miner. In January, he was called back to work, but when he went for the company physical, he failed it because he had hypertension. He made an appointment to see a doctor, but had a heart attack before he could go. In the hospital, he found out that the attack was minor and received medication. Two weeks ago he passed his second company physical. He was to report to work on a Monday, but instead he had a massive coronary over the weekend at home and died.

The man was forty-two. My student's mother has been out of work for six months because she was in a car accident and can barely walk. My student and her mother are going on welfare and food stamps. Her father had a small life insurance policy, and they would have gotten a death benefit from the company, but remember, he had only passed his physical; he had not actually returned to work at the mine, so technically he wasn't an employee. My student and her mother could lose their house. Michael, this student is already working part time and going to school full time, but even that could be in jeopardy.

As my student and I talked, I saw in the ways her eyes tightened and her voice hardened that she sees the company as the enemy. In fact, I have heard the same tone from other children of miners—and ex-miners themselves—a level of anger that resonates with the years of strain and conflict between the union and the mine owners. I'm going to the financial aid office to find out how she can get the help she needs to stay in school.

Mark

Mark:

Although some of my students may seem tougher than the miner's daughter you mentioned, they're just as shaky inside, just as filled by strains and pain. Suicides and homicides and too often no one reliable beside them. It's a flipping miracle they ever make it as far as the threshold of our classrooms, that they set themselves down and open themselves up and hold up their heads and hands and eyelids and spirits long enough—sometimes imperceptibly—to catch even just a little bit of the "something" that might change their lives for the better. And in such a moment, what can I give? Only everything and it's never going to be enough.

Michael

Mark:

I'm reading in James Howard Kunstler's *The Geography of Nowhere* and thinking about my students and their homes. I'm thinking about how often students will write and/or speak of their homes as places to stay away from, their neighborhoods as places to beware of. Kunstler writes:

> Quickest to uproot themselves are the educated classes, generally to advance their corporate careers. In an earlier era, these would have been the people who stayed put long enough to become stewards, official or otherwise, of that complex of values known as pride of place. They would have owned the business blocks downtown, and taken care of them. They would have built the churches, the libraries, the town bandshell, the ballfields. And they would have built houses for their own families that embodied the ideas of endurance and continuity. Today, this class of citizen is in the service of the large corporations whose very survival is predicated on destroying local economies and thus local communities. So it is somehow just that their hirelings should live in places of no character, no history, and no community. (148–49)

I'm struck, in particular, by Kunstler's remark about building things that "embodied the ideas of endurance and continuity." The communities with which I deal most frequently—housing projects, urban neighborhoods, my own community in Carroll Gardens, Brooklyn, provide interesting evidence for Kunstler's claim. In the housing projects, for example, people live in buildings that *were* designed and built for endurance and continuity. For the most part, urban housing projects were built by and for the working class: factory workers, machinists, people in the trades, laborers, and so on. And yet, the residents there now are often the city's poorest, those without jobs, single-parent families, and of course, as "everyone knows," most of the people in NYC's housing projects are Black or Latino. They are living in housing intended to last a lifetime, but enjoying very little of that enduring quality, that sense of continuity reflected in the design. Instead, the city's agencies regard residents of housing projects as second-class citizens. Evidence for this is visible: the city doesn't replace or repair light fixtures, doesn't provide suffi-cient police presence, doesn't maintain the buildings and grounds, plumbing and heating are poorly maintained and serviced, and large numbers of the residents are likely to be unemployed, on public assistance, or employed at low-income jobs.

Imagine how difficult it is for anyone to feel any particular pride in their neighborhood when that neighborhood feels like something from which to escape. Imagine the irony the kids experience when they learn that inmates in the area jails and correctional facilities have more amenities than their homes do. Of course, jail is jail. It is not home. You cannot just walk out of jail into the streets. But I can't tell you how many of my students, some of whom have family members currently in prison, complain about inmates having more luxuries and privileges than they do.

It is common to hear gunfire every night in the projects. The Gowanus Projects, eight blocks from my apartment, frequently have some kind of gun-related crime committed on the grounds or in one of the units. There are always cops with lights (and sometimes sirens) careening down Hoyt street or up Smith or down Bond street on their way to shoot it out with someone who could neither put up nor shut up with the ways things are. I'm not being a bleeding heart, Mark. I just know that the levels of meanness and cruelty in this city are in direct proportion to the meanness and cruelty demonstrated from the "top" down, from the Governor to the mayor, to local politicians and law-enforcement. In too many places and ways in this city you could not buy an ounce of dignity, a gram of safety, for all the money in Governor Pataki's retirement fund.

Michael

Michael:

The response I would offer is a mixture of sardonic anger and spiritual anguish. The people in the housing projects you write about are not supposed to endure. Witness the entire lack of government and business leadership in economic development, health care, and safety in and around the housing projects and for the people of which you speak.

You can't buy dignity, but some of our students sure do earn it. I recently received a book, an autobiography, from one of my Philadelphia students. He recounts witnessing two murders, and he tells of several family members being killed. The book ends with his decision to come to school to become an elementary teacher to do so some good for inner city children.

My rural and small-town working class white students are also forgotten, in a different way. Their hopelessness testifies to another kind of neglect: since they offer no lucrative services in the emerging nomadic/moneyed world order so aptly described by Jacques Attali, they are expendable. Alcohol abuse seems rampant among them. Why is it that the one business that is omnipresent in the Western PA small towns I drive through is the local tavern? There may be nothing else: no grocery, no hardware, no gas station. But there will be a tavern. The coal mines may be gone, and the steel mills in cities of larger populations may be gone, but there will be a tavern.

The American mythos includes the idea that rural folks are surrounded by natural beauty—space. The fact is that many of my rural students are awash in boredom and beer.

Michael, there is so much strain in these students. I don't want to argue that all of our students are emotional time bombs or that the only thing I do as a composition teacher is to elicit narratives of pain. But these narratives pile up anyway. Do you know how often someone in my composition classes ends up crying? Sometimes I think there's something wrong with a class in which this happens; then I think that there's something wrong with a culture in which this happens.

Mark

_____

Mark:

You are right—the people of the projects are not supposed to survive—they're not "fit." If they were, they'd be "movin' on up . . . to the East Side . . . to that deeeluxe apartment in the sky. . . ." And I should not limit culpability to the State of New York. Clinton's welfare "reform" concessions can only bring about more suffering, more alienation. My students know that people on welfare cannot simply "get" jobs, and the jobs they get do not pay the rent. And if they can pay the rent, they cannot afford child care for the little ones. And if they can afford child care, they can't afford clothes or food. Yes, there are food stamps, but for how long?

There are just so many young mothers in New York City—everywhere, really—who don't have a chance to enjoy anything close to peace of mind, security, safety. They are worrying about feeding the kids, about not being murdered or raped, about landlords throwing them out, about their own families giving up on them, about a government that is *not* "for" the people unless the people can pay for it, and they're worried about their own abilities to stay healthy enough to care for children they are, too often, raising alone. I still hear, too goddamn often, "Well, why are these girls having babies? They should know better! They bring it on themselves." And I keep thinking, why are these *boys* and *men* making these babies? Why don't *they* know better? I think, too, that such questions seem limp in the face of things that need to be done.

The word "rural" has always brought to my mind images of tract housing, rusted cars in someone's yard, too intimate a knowledge of one's neighbors' activities, listlessness. So, I can immediately grasp what you say about the boredom and the beer. There *is* space and beauty, and even a bit of nature left to some folks in this country. The fact that too many people seem to have lost a sense of knowing what to do in these spaces is disturbing to say the least. And I'm not sure that being well-educated in arts and letters makes people more able to cope with the boredom and silence of rural life. Why *is* it boring to live in a rural place? What has happened that being surrounded by space and trees, animals and sky could seem so dull? What expectations have been soaked into every one of us, in cities and towns, villages, hamlets, and addresses unknown?

As for your class and crying students: you know, this well does not dry up. There are tears that bubble up from springs that started generations ago. So, what are we doing, Mark? What do you do when Roland cries? You comfort him . . . maybe distract him . . . remind him of the good things that might outweigh the sadness or frustration of the moment . . . you listen, sure, but you also tell him things . . . I'm actually projecting, now. These are the things I do with Daina and Cory. When Daina cries, not quite knowing why, I have had to learn how to hold her without asking questions, how to be patient for the telling that might come, and how to know—or to guess—the one or two questions I might ask that can help her to untangle a knot of troubles. And then, when she tries to tell me that she misses me during the week, that maybe her mother didn't listen to her when she tried to explain why she did something, that she doesn't understand, still, after four years, why I don't live with them, I have to try not to let my own tears drown her. I have to figure out how to listen and to explain things in ways that are honest *and* gentle. And I have to urge her to try to give her own explanations of these things so I can see and hear how she is composing her life and her problems. If I don't keep these lines fully open between us, I know she will suffer in a frustrated silence.

But is this what I'm to do in the classroom, too? I don't think so, actually. And yet, sometimes, this is more or less what seems to be happening as our students write their way into (and sometimes out of) their troubles.

Is there a gentle way to say that I don't really want to be the parent to my students? I want to hear them out, to listen, to help them explain and compose themselves, their ideas, their links to and through knowledge, but I also *don't* want to limit their classroom experience to a grand counseling session.

Michael

———————————

Michael:

I absolutely agree. We are not running, as you say, counseling sessions. We are not qualified, and that is not the work our students come to us to do.

Daina—yes, it is a constant learning lesson just to figure out how to console our children. Sometimes all our advanced degrees in rhetoric do not help enough—OK, many times—OK, all the time.

Mark

_____

Mark:

We talk about upheavals in the lives of our students. I'm thinking again about Elspeth Stuckey's point about how important it is for us to consider where and who we're from. How many of your students have told you about their families as a way of trying to explain why they say what they say or why they feel the way they do about the world? I know the answer: plenty. Me, too. And what about us? Here's something:

I saw my father on Saturday at my sister's. He did not expect to see me any more than I did him. It's been a year since last contact, also accidental. He seemed nervous to find me there. My father couldn't stop staring at my kids and trying to engage them in clever repartee. Daina was openly perplexed when she heard me sigh, "Hi, Dad," and wanted to know who this guy was. I explained that one of the "Grandpas" that Daina hears her cousins talking about is this man, here. I had to explain that the man I think of as my dad, the one she knows as her grandfather, is my stepfather. Then came the inevitable question about whether, when her mother remarries, I will remain her real dad.

Mark, since 1976, I have seen my father perhaps a dozen times; since 1982, I've seen him three times and spoken to him one additional time. A long history of strain, of his violent outbursts when my sisters and I were kids, of the open hostilities and aggressive acts between my mother and father after their divorce, and his refusal as of '82 to hear from children he believed had slighted him one too many times, have all contributed to this gulf between us. And somehow, these sentences do nothing to explain the shattering effects that my father's actions have had on my sisters and me. There has been too much poison between my father and me (you know how these sorts of things work). And so, even now, it is a strain to see him, to think about him, to be in the same room with him, to fight back the combination of agitation and anger and, strangely, longing I feel when I even think about him because now I think I can understand a little bit of what his rages were about. My father and I have, quite literally, lost a lifetime between us. I don't know, Mark. Lately, I feel I need to build a bridge, however rickety. I'm thinking of writing to him—at least we can open up a channel of communication that we can both control.

Is it ridiculous of me to try to imagine what I would tell a student who might come to me describing this situation? Probably I would mostly listen; maybe that's what I need to do—listen to myself to figure out what I need to do. And probably I would suggest writing a letter, to build a bridge while it's still possible.

Michael

———————————

Michael:

It's so strange about your father. It must have been head-spinning to run into him like that—and for your kids. So many adults walk in and out of our kids' lives—how disrupting to the sense of things.

I offer you a lot of advice lately, but here goes again: make the contact with him and do the soul-healing necessary gestures. And accept what little honest connection to something larger than yourself that he can offer, and keep the best part of yourself safe from him (I know you know all of this—there is no new wisdom in these matters.)

Fathers.

I've told you how one of my earliest memories of my father is seeing him beat up my mother. How she stayed by him through his affairs, drunkenness, drug addiction, and cruelty. And how late in life they grew close.

He was a troubled man, yet he was capable of great love. One of my best later memories of him was how he stayed up all night with me once when I was in high school and had the flu. I remember how gentle his touch was as he laid his hand on my forehead to feel for fever. I don't think I can reconcile both kinds of memories of that hand.

Mark

———————————

Mark:

In the coolest, most detached voice you could conjure, one of my students read aloud from his composition on the meanings of "hanging out." He told us that in the 13 years or so that he's been hanging out on one particular Brooklyn street corner (mind you, he's 18, so his hanging out days started when he was around 5), he's *seen* a murder, a sexual assault, "a lot of shootings," and a number of incidents that he described as police brutality. What was even more eye-opening was that he listed other things he'd seen that he said "can't be classified." These included one guy sticking a screw-driver in another guy's eye. He said that these guys were "friends" who just "got into it" this one time. Another time he helped a friend hold a man down on the sidewalk while a third friend "kicked the guy's head in" because the guy had "dissed" the kids who were hanging out. And he told us about how he and his friends used to fill their water-guns with bleach and shoot them into passing cars hoping to blind the drivers and cause accidents.

Students—far too many students—laughed.

Michael

Michael:

Some nights I wake up in a cold sweat wondering if we have the right to tell the stories we are trying to in *Letters*. Our students are so encouraging in their willingness to allow these narratives—even cloaked in editorial protection—but I just wonder.

Yet, I know the value. First, these stories sometimes seem to be the only ones worth telling because they are the most necessary ones to tell, they are the ones that matter. If we continue to teach composition, with student-centeredness and personal experience—however we connect the personal to the social—at the heart of the thing, we surely must compose something that honestly addresses the pain at the center of some student experience and composing. In addition, we must investigate, with students, the connection of that pain to the social injustices that cause it. If our students speak of their pain in their compositions, we simply cannot ignore it. And even if we try to ignore it or legislate against it by making assignments designed to ban the personal from school writing, the pain will still be there in other terms, in its own terms.

Second, I know we both agree that these stories have the potential to move some, if not all, in the profession into doing things differently. Cultural studies and composition studies people, for instance, might turn their attention from theoretical abstractions of student experience and composing (such as "subject positions"), ones which diminish the qualities of the living, and learn about the connection of the composing to the living. Gertrude Stein said it about artists, and it applies to our students: ". . . they are conducting life and that makes their composition what it is, makes their work compose as it does" (517). Connecting the living and the composing to the theoretical concerns of cultural issues might lead us to some significant questions: what lives are our students conducting? what makes our students' compositions what they are? what makes their work compose as it does? how does it compose? what or whom is it composing? who is listening? how is the audience responding? how do the audience members conduct their lives from now on? what does the audience compose? As I think about these questions, I realize they are more than a beginning. They are one outline for a curriculum, for a philosophy of teaching, for a socially responsible teaching project to which one can meaningfully dedicate oneself.

Mark

Mark:

We will tell the stories we will tell because:

1. They are real.
2. The stories and the tellers occupy and preoccupy us.
3. Some of them need (re)telling—they are too volatile, too strained, too dangerous to keep silent. Our culture seems to value privacy less and less. But, to keep "private" about the violence and the peace (or efforts to find or make peace) is also to continue the pretense that such things are not integrally part of life at school—and of course at home.

Michael

Michael:

Look, we are also telling these stories for ourselves. We are telling these stories to try to make our own lives make sense. In her study of the linguistics of narrative, *Life Stories*, Charlotte Linde points out how people tell their stories as much to make a kind of coherence out of their lives, to prove that life and experience have meaning, as to make a text for social consumption (16–18). But too often our time as teachers seems so chaotic, too full of a multitude of half-told tales and lessons forgotten from the end of one semester to the beginning of the next.

Who writes the stories down? Who writes enough of them down? Who hears them and says what they mean? What do they mean? What does anyone mean in the middle of so many? What gets lost when they didn't know they could write them down? No one told them they were worth writing down. Worth saying what they mean. How can we not write them down?

Michael, a few semesters ago a wonderful student wrote a healing book, *Tending the Flame*, for one of my Advanced Composition classes. *Tending the Flame* is about the death of her twenty-one-year-old brother. The book is filled with a variety of parts: a section for other teenagers suggesting ways to survive the loss of a family member, to help make others "feel a little less isolated, a little less alone"; a section on the writer's own grief: "For awhile you begin to think that you're special—like maybe you belong to an exclusive little club. Perhaps you understand things others don't and your experience has made you 'wise.' But then you begin to realize that death is something that happens"; a section on what she has learned: "it's no longer so easy to take the lives and love of those close to me for granted"; and a section of all the things she wishes she could tell her brother: "Why didn't I ever tell you? I don't know for sure. I suppose I thought I had all the time in the world and that someday you'd know all these things."

CCCC after CCCC, you have complained to me, Michael, that we and our profession are no closer to knowing what we need to know. We need to know how to help our students to write the stories down. For example, we need to tell anyone who will listen—and even those who will try not to—what we learn from our students about taking a stand in the face of violence. They have stories. They are made of stories. They're even left out of stories that purport to be about them. If we're going to say anything about the social whole, we had better make room for the whole story.

I can imagine how someone might say that this is an outdated model of teaching as nurturing. I think I know how you would respond, though, Michael: our students seem to receive so little nurturing, so little of the basic attentions. We don't mind renewing some kind of call for care in our writing classrooms.

Mark

Teachers *should* be good listeners, and good readers, but do we know what we should be listening for? What words have we taught our students to say? What sounds have we taught them to make?

We are arguing that teachers must, at *least*, become better listeners and readers. We know that the amount of material we all must look at and evaluate can be daunting. But if we are going to ask students to write and to "participate," which typically means to raise their hands and to respond orally to class discussion, we ought to know what they are talking about and to understand the places from which their remarks are coming. Margo Wilson and Martin Daly note that "violence is often the recourse of desperate people lacking access to the positive incentives that might inspire more 'voluntary' compliance" (120). They add that hostilities and conflicts arise and escalate when people feel they cannot effectively negotiate with one another to get even basic needs met (120). We ought to know a lot more than we do about the conflicts and personal struggles our students face and about how they meet these conflicts.

Mark:

Sometimes I read a passage that is so completely itself in itself, folded in, gesturing toward me, not needing me, connected to everything I have been thinking, absolutely separate from *my* thinking, and I realize that this has always been one of the deepest pleasures in reading, the intangible thing I want so much to convey to my children—although I see it happening already in Daina when she reads something "cool" in Shel Silverstein, or in H. D.'s *The Hedgehog*. It's what I want to show, to give, to teach my students—this pleasure. Yesterday, the pleasure came, ironically, in the form of a terrible ache when I read one particular passage in J. M. Coetzee's *In the Heart of the Country*. In this book, a young woman lives on a farm in South Africa, far from others, with her father and his new young bride. The narrative consists of 266 diary entries by the young woman who has, we learn quickly, been raped by her father when she was very young and who has never been able to recover her equilibrium. Early in the narrative, we see, already, that she has, according to her increasingly disturbing and disturbed diary entries, murdered her father and his wife in their bed and now must dispose of the bodies and cleanse the house before the housekeeper and servants discover what has happened.

Before the double-murder, she stands alone in her tiny room at night and "records" the following:

> What are pain, jealousy, loneliness doing in the African night? Does a woman looking through a window into the dark mean anything? I place all ten fingertips on the cool glass. The wound in my chest slides open. If I am an emblem then I am an emblem. I am incomplete, I am a being with a hole inside me, I signify something, I do not know what, I am dumb, I stare out through a sheet of glass into a darkness that is complete, that lives in itself, bats, bushes, predators and all, that does not regard me, that is blind, that does not signify but merely is. If I press harder the glass will break, blood will drip, the cricket-song will stop for a moment and then resume. I live inside a skin inside a house. There is no act I know of that will liberate me into the world. There is no act I know of that will bring the world into me. I am a torrent of sound streaming into the universe, thousands upon thousands of corpuscles weeping, groaning, gnashing their teeth. (Coetzee 9–10)

It's hard not to transpose some of this eloquent, awful silence to some of the lives you and I have encountered in our years at JJC and IUP. Do you remember when I wrote to you about a class in which I'd learned that so many of the women had been sexually abused by a family member, generally the father, and that I was shocked not only at the number, but at the almost terrible blend of candor and pain they expressed in their poetry? And do you recall that the majority of these women were from the Caribbean? When I spoke with a colleague from the African-American Studies department, she told me it did not surprise her at all to know how frequent such childhood rapes-by-fathers are, and she, rightly, warned me to be very careful in how I dealt with such revelations, no matter how unsolicited they had been. I told her that I thought I would say something about it—as I am doing here—in the book I was writing. She said, "Yes, say something about it. Do it carefully. Give no names, but do say something." I am saying something, but is saying "something" sufficient?

How *does* one deal with such revelations, Mark? I've been referring people to counselors, shelters, our Women's Center, the police (if they preferred), lawyers, for years, and I keep on asking friends and colleagues this question: how can I best be helpful and supportive to those who even hint at such pain?

Coetzee's passage seems to give a "voice" to an ache of loneliness so deep, a despair so complete. I know such moments in literature are precisely the "magic" of the written word.

Michael

Michael:

I can't help but want to answer your questions, maybe for myself as much as for you. But more for our students, of course. Yes, we can start by referring our students to the people qualified to help them when they are in difficulty. That is a significant beginning. We both know that. Are there times when we can do more? should do no more? are we missing the most important things that we could do? Perhaps so—and I hope not.

Listen to this from Sharon Sutton as she writes about the power of creative pedagogies, or teaching through the arts: "What kind of learning processes would tap into the magic of power-from-within, which can rupture the fabric of old beliefs and allegiances? How could we use that magic to construct new personal and societal identities—new mental maps of sustainability?" (208).

I think that the value of our writing back and forth to each other—well, one value anyway—is the way we keep telling each other, even in the face of our tremendous felt need to articulate answers, that we need to begin and even stay in the questions we raise. For Sandra Hollingsworth (230) staying in the questions is a commitment to keeping things open, to resisting the totalizing myths and foreclosures of disciplinary conclusions.

Don't we ask students to write about what they *need* to write about because we believe it does some kind of good to give testimony to the legitimacy of their lives? What changes our pedagogies offer in the actual lived conditions of our students' lives is of course another matter. To what extent can we and our students write to find the "magic" we need to construct "new mental maps of sustainability"; that is, what is the connection between the writing our students do and the construction of new identities that are not only sustain-able, but conservative of health and our planet?

I told you about Karen, who was missing class because she had been in the hospital? She came to class earlier this week with her doctor's excuse, and, after class, she told me that the reason she was in the hospital was that she had tried to kill herself. She said her therapist was helping her, but that she couldn't really explain her actions. I asked if she was OK, thinking as I spoke that "I don't know what to say." She said she was still "shaky," but that she was working on her book for class, a book about herself that she intended as a warning to others to tell them not to do what she had done. I asked if there was anything I could do, again thinking, "*Is* there anything I *can* do?" She said no. She didn't come to class yesterday. (I will of course look into what's happened.) So, yes, are there times when we can do more? should do no more? are we missing the most important things that we could do? Perhaps. Probably? So we need to stay in our questions.

Mark

Mark:

I'm still at work—have been here since 8 AM. Now it's nearly 8 PM. One of my students is a former Corrections Officer. Years back he was told by a couple of captains and some superiors to beat the hell out of a child-molester, which he felt he had to agree to do. So he set it up and then, in front of some of those superiors, the guy was beaten within an inch of his life. Turned out, the guy was proved innocent, sued the state and won 500K. My student turned state's evidence to keep himself out of prison, and now must live with the knowledge of what he'd done.

He says, now, that if he could live it all over again, he'd say "NO" to his superiors and take the consequences, but he also knows that, at that time, he felt powerless to resist.

Michael

Michael:

I lost the student who thinks it's a good day for genocide against homosexuals. He finished the course, but he wrote me a note about how he felt that I had never understood him. I wonder if there ever was a chance for us to understand each other. He came with too much anger. I don't think I was prepared for that much violence expressed so secretly and intensely.

Mark

Mark:

A student I told you about last semester—she'd been in a fiction-writing class and had written about escaping a violent domestic partner—came to visit me this afternoon. On her forehead was a kind of circular scar from stitches. She told me her (new) boyfriend had hit her in the head with a screwdriver and had opened it up. She said she was "OK" now, but that she didn't plan to have any more boyfriends for a while.

Michael

_____

Michael:

Roland will be an extra on an upcoming *Mr. Rogers' Neighborhood* entitled something like, "What To Do With Your Hands When You Feel Like Hitting Someone."

What to do indeed.

Ro told me today that he does not want to see *Pocahontas* because, as he said, people get shot in it.

Mark

_____

Mark:

My students sometimes come back, sometimes years later, but many of them just disappear into the urban darkness. I have a student this summer whose older brother was in a remedial class I taught at least 6 years ago. The older brother used to come to my office to look at my books. It was funny, he liked to read the titles, ask me about them, his questions got more and more interesting, and then he'd tell me about his life (though he didn't mention his younger brother that I recall). He'd been raised by an aunt, his parents died young in Puerto Rico, and he'd been mainly working the streets, small-time, scared. So he came to college, struggled through a year and a half of failure and ended up in my basic writing class. He did OK. He passed and came around a few times the following term. He still liked to look at my books. Finally I gave him an anthology of Modern Literature and also a copy of a poetry anthology by Latin American poets.

So now his younger brother is in my class. He told me his older brother had me as a teacher; he remembered my last name. I asked him how his older brother is. He said, "Oh, he died. He got shot. Workin' the streets, man. They kill you out there." He said it like he was recalling a newspaper article. I told him I was sorry. He said, "Yeah, it's OK. Thanks. Shit like that happens, you know? He took a chance."

The sad thing, in addition, is that the younger brother is a very poor student. He misses class a lot, hands in work done carelessly (when it's done at all), and doesn't seem to care about anything. I suggested he come by to talk; he said he would "some time maybe" as though he were offering the hope to me.

Schools are like poorly made nets. We catch a few—the easily caught ones—and then we don't know what to do with them. We sure don't know what to do about all the ones that get away. But we keep replacing the net because we cannot imagine any other thing to do.

The older brother was about 22 when he died. His younger brother is 22 right now. These kids live on top of volcanoes.

Michael

Michael:

I wonder what would happen if we were to trade places for a week. I am very far from New York City life, especially as it is experienced by your students. I doubt I would know how to hear the things that either of the brothers in your e-mail would tell me. I might want to "be there" for them in a sympathetic way, but how would they respond? And how would I deal with the "newspaper article" account by the younger brother of the older brother's death? And for god's sake, what would I do with the kinds of stories the younger brother could tell me about life—and death—on New York's streets?

I try to picture you in my office meeting my students as I do. What would you make of the experiences of my mining and steel family students? You are far from rural and small-town life. Still, if our students endure so many similar kinds of violence—the various forms of sexual violence for instance—despite differences in locale, family, and so on, isn't there some kind of common link we can see here? some way by which we can get our bearings as we try to respond in some adequate fashion to what our students tell us?

Your student says, "Oh he died. He got shot. Shit like that happens." My students from mining families say, "Oh yeah, we all lose someone in the mines. An uncle or a brother, your father, someone. We all know that." They share a certain resignation—or is it stoicism or toughness or what?

I wonder in what sense we are even teaching the same things. We keep calling it "composition," but I keep wondering about the things our students are composing. We keep talking about building links among our students so that they can enter into healthy collaborations. Isn't there one here that we need to explore?

Mark

How can you believe us? How can it be that there are so many tales of violence and pain in our classrooms? Even statistically speaking, how can it be? Sometimes we can hardly believe it ourselves. But that is exactly the right first question to ask: how can it be? Has it always been this way? Did we fail to see it before? Do teachers fail to see it now? How can we have failed to see the violence if it is so prevalent both in our New York City classroom with its urban students and our western Pennsylvanian classroom with its rural, small-town, and midwestern urban students? What were we looking at when we missed it?

Why, and how, have our students come to write these things in our courses? We have chosen to make our pedagogies an extension of our commitment to the value of correspondence between caring people. Our students know we care about them, and their writings are always, in part, one-half of a correspondence, the other half of which is our responsibility and our privilege. And their writings are also part of the correspondence that anyone—everyone—ought to feel part of in their negotiations in and with the world. We know that's pretty high flown, and most people do not feel inclined or able to do this. But isn't that what we're supposed to facilitate in our classes? Students come to our courses expecting to learn things that will (further) connect them to one another and to the social whole, fragmented though it is.

What else do they expect of us? And what can we expect from ourselves? Can we possibly talk about higher education without thinking that our work must have something to do with alternatives to the violence we have been discussing? We began *Letters for the Living* by arguing that the teaching of writing has everything to do with both violence *and* peace. Is this only a half-truth?

Introduction to Part 3

Mark:

I have just returned from a bike ride in Prospect Park during which I was listening to bird calls and songs, to whizzed-by fragments of lovers' conversations as they walked the same loop, noticing how many people seem to be moving about the undergrowth, emerging from heavily wooded areas with variously hidden faces and downcast eyes.

I could smell a dozen different bits of evidence that a spring rain is decidedly different than a winter rain. I could feel the temperature of the air change as I moved through high ground to the lower east end of the loop where the lake cools the air and draws kids and their fishing rods. For a few miles, another cyclist and I, after an initial greeting, rode together in silence, satisfied that the pace was good. And somewhere halfway down my lifetime, my body was remembering having felt fine—maybe not so trim anymore, maybe not so quick to change its geometry, but my hands and face and legs and the top of my head all knew that it must be possible to feel restored.

Michael

3 Peace

Consider the will to love
as the decision to survive.

—Gloria Frym, "Training for the Apocalypse"

And why do I write? Garcia Marquez once said that he writes so
that his friends will love him more. I think I write so that people
will love each other more.

—Isabel Allende, "Writing as an Act of Hope"

Maybe there can be no peace. We don't imagine anything we do in a
classroom or for a group of students is going to stop the violence or
bring about peace. No, that's not true. We imagine it all the time. But it's
not happening, is it?

In *The Violence of Literacy*, J. Elspeth Stuckey wonders

> What to do with our profession, what to do with our mechanisms of
> oppression, what to do with our hysteria or complacency or resig-
> nation, what to do with the great disparities among our resources
> and knowledge and access to help, what to do with a world whose
> literacy pampers us but targets those we teach, what to do with a
> violent history, a miserly present, and a myopic future? What to
> do—we English teachers—to deal with all that? (124)

Some days, it seems so simple and clear. Maybe it's because we have
children that we know, absolutely, that we cannot throw in the towel
and say, "There can be no peace; there is no peace." What is the point of
teaching people to read and write if we are not also trying to teach them
to understand the world and to make it better? One answer Stuckey
offers is that "It may be that the most likely way change will ever happen is incremental, local, one person at a time" (126). And by what incremental methods can we deal with the violence that, as Stuckey argues,
constitutes the "incremental, daily violence against those who are not
favored by the system" (127)? We would say that teachers are already
dealing with "it."

What if peace, wherever it is, however fragile and transitory it may be, what if that peace depends upon a constant, incremental, local, personal vigil kept by the handfuls and communities full of people who believe that it is not only possible but necessary to live in peace? The easiest thing to forget is that you have to *make* peace. Maybe the second easiest thing to do, in this regard, is to fail to notice or to pay attention to the moments of peace when they happen. We may feel we cannot find peace because there is simply too much noise, too much rushing us, too much distracting us. And perhaps it seems unfair to feel and enjoy moments of peace when we are aware of the violence and suffering that is occurring as near as next door and as far away as on the evening news. What can peace be for someone who is learning about the atrocities of war and neglect, of economic and cultural collapse, of the disappearance of freedom throughout the world? What can peace mean to someone living through such things? Still, what is living without the hearing, seeing, and recognizing of moments of peace? Hopelessness? The loss of the hope that sustains us when we try to build communities? The loss of the hope that drives us to search out nourishing forms of intimacy?

We think so. But in a chapter entitled "Peace," we are hesitant to argue that we have found or created some sort of peaceable system in which to raise our kids, to live in our communities, or to do our work.

Michael:

I have an undergraduate student in my writing class who told me that she is repeating the course because last semester she received the grade of F. Now I know this student to be energetic, bright, able, and cooperative, so I asked her what had happened. How could she, I wanted to know, ever have failed this writing class? She explained to me that right near the end of the semester, she had suffered a terrible tragedy. Her infant son had died in an accident at home—he had drowned, I take it, during his bath. Of course, she missed class time and, as I said, it was right near the end of the semester. My student went to her professor and explained what had happened. She asked him for an incomplete so that she could make up the work she had missed. The professor said no. I don't know what motivated this professor to this decision.

I mourn for my student's loss. This student is doing fine work in my course. Outside of class, she has asked for some suggestions for an article she is writing to submit to a magazine on parenting so that her tragedy might stand as a lesson for other parents.

Mark

Here's a woman who has faced the most outrageous personal tragedy we can think of. And in the face of this tragedy, she has chosen to
care about people she has never met. We want to be sure to draw attention to such gestures and to learn all we can from them. They must shape
our lives and work as much as—no, far more than—violence does. But
making—and educating for—peace requires us to understand what *peace*
means. Can we define *peace* by way of moments of lived experience?
Moments where we think peace is what's happening? Betty A. Reardon
writes, in *Comprehensive Peace Education: Education for Global Responsibility,* "Peace is problematic not only as a goal but even as a concept. Popular wisdom has often held that peace is unachievable because it is
indefinable" (13). Can we begin to give peace a living definition? Is educating for peace simply another way teachers teach abstractions about a
world that does not exist?

> If . . . we are going to work seriously for peace, we are going to have
> to rethink some of the values and beliefs that are at the core of our
> society, which help to glorify conquest and mastery. . . . But how do
> we begin to rethink? And how do we teach the whole society to
> reeducate itself? (Brock-Utne, *Educating for Peace: A Feminist Perspec-
> tive* 72)

How indeed? Perhaps the start of an answer lies in an approach to
teaching where students can learn to see themselves in what Reardon
calls their "planetary stewardship" (*Women and Peace* 132). They, and
we, are responsible for the planet. That means we are responsible for
one another, as well. This doesn't only mean we must educate on a global scale, whatever that might entail: "We must be equally determined
to end the oppression of any one individual by another" (Brock-Utne
73). Peace begins at home. We know, we know; you have read words
like this before. How does it work? How do we begin? Perhaps as we do
in this book, by attending, first, to violence—to pain. In a 1989 interview
with Gloria Watson, bell hooks said, "I say remember the pain because I
believe true resistance begins with people confronting pain, whether
it's theirs or somebody else's, and wanting to do something to change it.
And it's this pain that so much makes its mark in daily life" ("An Interview" 215). hooks says we have to remember the pain—and from this,
we understand that we must remember the everyday suffering every
day. Then peace, too, we would argue, is an everyday thing—meaning,
we have to figure it out every day. But we said "no more pretending."
The truth is that many days, we simply can't figure out either the pain
or the peace. In *The Culture of Pain*, David B. Morris writes,

> Pain passes much of its time in utter inhuman silence, and writers
> who describe something so inherently resistant to language must
> inevitably shape and possibly falsify the experience they describe.

There is no completely pure or innocent account of pain untouched by the constraints of writing—including scientific writing. Yet writers also offer a unique resource because they use language in ways that, paradoxically, acknowledge (without necessarily falsifying) the silences and inarticulate struggles we most often completely overlook. But they do more. They also allow us to examine various moments—specific historical junctures—when pain thrusts above the plane of silent, blind, unquestioned suffering in which it ordinarily lies concealed. Because pain leads its existence mostly in secret, in silence, without leaving written records or eloquent testimony, our main evidence in documenting the historical life of pain lies in fragmentary episodes and in scattered moments. Such fragments nonetheless prove fully adequate to support the claim that what surgeon René Leriche in 1937 aptly called "living pain"—pain experienced outside the laboratory and not reduced to a universal code of neural impulses—always contains at its heart the human encounter with meaning. (3)

So, even if the suffering and pain of life are the hardest of experiences to articulate, Morris points to the value of the writing. For us, as teachers of writing, his words affirm the value of our students' "scattered moments," and the "fragmentary episodes" that document not only pain, but also triumphs as profound as any we find in literature. These writings foreground the stubborn silences in which pain often operates. This foregrounding calls for the creating of intimacy—the sharing of pain and understanding and the community that can arise in the process of this sharing. *Intimacy.* Such an odd word to use to describe a possible requirement for work in a composition class. Intimacy. In the middle of a semester, in the middle of a curriculum, in the middle of a school or university, in the middle of a city or country—in the middle of life. Yet intimacy and community—and peace—are exactly what the living composing is about: the needs that each of us has; the needs that the most stubborn of silences addresses.

Michael:

I am thinking about Andrea, who will write about how her boyfriend beat her up (remember? She is the student who will miss time this semester so that she can get the medical attention she still needs).

Of course not all of my students write about such unhappy topics, but many do. Why? The assignment I give them asks them to write their books about what they are burning to tell the world, what they think the world needs to know. Some of them burn to tell the world about the kinds of violence they have seen or endured. Others decide to write about their loves, family, sports, or about courage in the face of tough circumstances. I try as hard as possible to let them know that these, too, can work as topics of their books.

Still, why do students decide to take up such hugely personal experiences in a class of strangers? Do students immediately recognize that these classrooms are safe places to do such important, sensitive, and honest work?

My guess is that our students' reasons for writing what they do are as varied as our students. But the more I talk to my students, the more I believe that they really are burning to tell their stories—to make sense—to make order and to validate. The student who wrote her book about her uncle's heroin over-dose cried as she told the class about the subject of her book. I said to her, "If this subject upsets you so much, you might not want to write about it for this class." She said, "No, I want to. In fact, my doctor told me that writing about it might help." She also said she is going to show the book to her doctor and maybe make it available for other patients who have lost a loved one to drugs.

Michael, I am reading the newest issue of *Creative Nonfiction* with my advanced composition class. There is a really moving piece, "A June Journal" by David Gessner. In it, Gessner writes about his father's impending death from cancer. The father has come to live his last weeks with his son. To prepare for his own death, the father works as hard as his limited strength will allow to put Gessner's house in order: overseeing lawn and garden work, stacking recyclable beer and soda cans. He is doing, one last time, for his son, and he is resisting death. The son is writing about the experience, recording it, also resisting his father's death. Both work more frantically as the end approaches. Gessner writes:

> I see him try to drag a lawn chair across the porch. I jump up and run downstairs to help him.
> Is this all there is to life? Is this what it is all about?
> Control. Is it as large an issue for everyone as we make it in our family? He is angry at his cancer. It's not at all under his control. And so he needs to control what he can. Dishes in the right place. Cans organized, etc.
> "Writing is breaking the illusion of control." This from the mother, a writer, of one of my students. Is it true? Or is writing also a way of putting things in their place? Metaphysically neatening up cans, organizing the unorganizable flux? (Gessner 55)

Teaching to help. To encourage writing and the making of understandings—however tentative, however inadequate. To provide occasions for students to create in order to take some kinds of control—perhaps only for a moment. To learn to exercise healing kinds of power.

Mark

————————————

Mark:

I think we prompt students to address and write about unhappy topics. It's not only us, though. Our students have grown up in an age where, when you scratch the polish off of someone you know or admire, you discover the knockout punch lurking beneath. When we ask students to write about something they feel the world "needs to know," they are probably figuring that the world all but ignores them most of the time, and that the surest way to be noticed and *listened to* is to tell the world something shocking, something dark or awful, something unexpectedly desperate. This doesn't mean the things they tell are any less real or disturbing. In fact, it's pretty damned disturbing to know how many of these stories there are in our students' lives. But there *is* something in the request to commit a revelation to paper that invites the stories most painful to tell and hear.

I doubt they recognize the safety element as quickly as you'd like to think, and you know I mean no disrespect to you, Mark. I'd say your students perceive a level of respect *from* you that they would like to have applied to their work as well. You may be, for some, the first professor, plain and simply, to respect them as intelligent writers who have important things to say. I also think our students are, increasingly, always on the precipice. They are right there at the threshold between silence and (finally) speaking their minds. Maybe this is the condition most of us are in. I don't know what my basis is for saying this except that I keep seeing and sensing it in my students—and maybe I sense it in myself, too. People have things to say and, too often, lack the words or the space, the permission or the perceived interest, the right moment in which to say them. Now I don't mean that we should encourage students to tell all. But the fact is we learn from their revelations—we gain insights, we grow as teachers, and we owe a great deal to what we are given each and every time one of our students allows us to know them slightly more than slightly. And I believe, to a perhaps limited extent, our students gain similarly when they can honestly realize we, too, have lives that can be considered and known.

More and more I want to find out, especially with my students, how they find and make *peace* within the lives they lead. How do they know how to bring peace to those around them when they, themselves, have known such a disproportionate amount of violence? I don't have to dig deep to learn about outrageous acts and sufferings of violence. What I have to learn how to do, and to do well, is to help students spin out their tales of peace and peacemaking. I don't want to create occasions of temporary control that they and I know are temporary and a little artificial. Well, one could argue that all forms of control are only temporary, but I mean to learn how to help start the engines that will then be able to keep refueling themselves.

Once again, the pipes in my apartment are making their death rattles—it's nearly impossible to concentrate, so I'll ease up, here. My radiators are leaking water. My office was flooded over the weekend (busted pipe), and so the water's everywhere, and rising. I guess you're going to want a place on the ark, eh?

Michael

Michael:

Besides the tragic books that shock and move us, I heard one student say that she was going to write a book about her immigrant grandfather and the soft drink business he started in one of the local hollows. Another is writing about three generations of women in her Philadelphia family: her grand-mother, her mother, and herself. Nearly every semester some student or two will say, after hearing about some of the tough situations some of the other students have endured, that they have nothing to write their books about because "Nothing bad has ever happened to me. My family is together. We love each other. No one is an alcoholic or abusive. I have not had cancer" etc. I have used such moments as opportunities to ask, if someone else doesn't do it first, "Why do you think that you have nothing to write a book about because nothing 'bad' has ever happened to you?" Or, now that I think about it, I remember one student saying, "You sound like you are apologizing because nothing tragic has happened to you. Perhaps you want to write how your family is happy, how they have maintained their happiness, or why you sound like you feel guilty about the fact that you have led a happy life." I don't remember her exact words, but that was the essence of the thing. A sharp response.

If you were to make my assignment with your students, would you get the books about love and health? You report the violence: Celia visiting her boyfriend in prison on Riker's Island, Gina writing about her disillusionment with being the girlfriend of a member of the gang.

I think that at least some of the students turn our respect for them into a feeling of safety. Last year one of my students said in class one day, "I don't feel like this class is a class. It's as if this class isn't part of the university—as if we were a club or something." Today one of my first-year composition students said, "We can write about anything we want in our books right? I mean we can write about anything we have done." The student from last year made me feel like the most successful writing teacher in the world—though I reminded her that this would be a graded club. We then discussed the problems posed by this fact. The student today scared me; I immediately reminded him that perhaps there was reason not to feel safe with making personal revelations to every other person in the room. He shook his head yes.

Mark

Mark:

I certainly don't disagree that your students feel safe. In fact, they may well feel that safety immediately upon taking their seats in your classroom. But I wonder, also, what *else* factors into a student's wanting to write "about anything" they "want in" their "books." One guess is that students have been led to believe that academic writing occurs in a vacuum. As risky as the subject matter may be, as good or bad as the grades have been thus far, the artifacts of composition they produce have had nowhere to go and nothing to do beyond showing up on their teachers' desks. And so, the idea that they can write anything isn't necessarily so radical. The idea that they can write anything and that it will be regarded as *important* and as part of a larger collective/collection of significant work(s) to be produced by your class—this makes the difference. Is this safety? Yes, it sure is. But it's more and/or something else, too.

You asked if my students would write books about "love and health." Interesting question. Some would, yes. But not without "permission" to do so. If I say, "Write a book about an important issue" (well, I *have* said this), they write about the things that move them. And I have to keep finding ways of suggesting, however subtly, that it's *OK* to yearn for peace and quiet, for love, for someone to take care of them, for someone to take care of.

In an in-class writing we did in a course called "Madness" [a Thematic Studies, interdisciplinary team-taught class, in this case, with a psychologist], students wrote a paragraph describing a form of "domestic" madness in lay terms. One woman wrote about the madness of constant noise. She's a single mother of two (at the time, a 3- and 5-year-old) who lives with her mother who's always on the phone yelling at someone. Her kids make lots of noise; she lives in the Bronx on a busy, noisy, unsafe street. The walls are thin, and she hears what's going on in the apartments above and beside her. The police and fire sirens are going all night long, as are the car alarms in the few moments before the cars are stolen or chopped. Somewhere there's always a dozen babies crying and a Doberman barking. Down below her third floor windows the boom boxes play Coolio or Snoop Doggy Dog all day and all night. And she wrote a sentence I am sad to love: "I know that it's madness to live like this and I know that when I die, I'll find my sanity."

Later in that period, when we'd heard a bunch of the paragraphs, she said something like "It's madness to hope somebody can come along and make your life all right, but maybe it's madness to stop hoping for it?" She'd put it as a question. I put it as a question. Mark, there aren't enough knights in shining armor, heroines, helping hands, or moments of silence to make all these lives all right. And yet, there she was, right there, among us, saying her piece, enjoying 3 hours of peace in which to speak or listen or just be part of something *for* her and her ideas.

I need to sleep—got to get up extra early to head out to Long Island to see Daina in a play (I'll bring Cory), then hustle back to the city to a meeting. Another night with less than four hours sleep . . . it's only January and already I'm tired.

Sheesh.

Michael

Michael:

You are right; our students have no doubt heard many times: "write about anything you like," which translates, most likely, as either: "here is your modicum of freedom, use it wisely" or "I don't have any ideas for this assignment so you figure something out." Nothing radical here.

I think the significant moment is when a class realizes that they have the right, wherewithal, creativity—the scholarly acumen and responsibility—to determine the research and writing agenda (within the context of this class). They have the same rights grad students may reasonably take for granted (though I may be presuming too much about the quality of the grad experience). Just imagine the disappointment, if not humiliation, students (I am thinking of undergrads here, though what I am about to say may apply elsewhere, too) must feel when they go to buy the books for their composition class and they see a handbook or a reader—even one of the glossy cultural studies readers. They know immediately that the teacher of this class has it all worked out: the subject matter, the assignments in sequence, the expectations, even the writing (I remember knowing something of these things, even as an undergrad, even through the haze of my skittish youth).

Mark

Michael:

You and I both take consolation from the fact that we can do things in writing. I suspect that finally it is the same for at least some of our students. Imagine that—after one of our classes, some of our students will know some of the things—control and creativity and power—about and from writing that keep *us* alive. They will experience some of *this* for themselves. Now or later.

Mark

Mark:

Your note reminds me that the difference(s) we make with students may not actually "happen" until pretty far down the road—a road we may never actually share or cross again with these students.

I want to tell you about George, a Vietnam vet who was in my Lit course. George would sit in his wheelchair down front, with his wife (who attended only to help her husband). His daughter was in the class after mine, so I met her, too. George decided early on that I was cool. He loved the fact that he was learning to love reading "this stuff," and he told me that he loved to see me hopping around the lecture room (with 60 students, I actually prepared lectures), telling them about Homer's *Odyssey* and about *Oedipus*.

George was often ill. His kidneys would shut down, sometimes his blood sugars would go haywire, and his lungs occasionally needed clearing, so he'd miss school. His wife told me that when he was sick, he'd tell her to be sure to attend my class and "record everything." She told me, also, that at a dinner party they'd had, he told a group of similarly disabled, Black vets, that he had a teacher who "makes you want to crawl up into his words": a quote, Mark, I cannot forget.

Recently George won a fairly sizable fellowship for graduate studies, and I'd written one of the recommendation letters. When he won, he called me up at home and wept. He said, "We did it, man, we did it!" I said, "*You* did it, George." He said, "No, man, you got this way of making me feel like I got the *Power*!" I had to laugh as potential TV ministries swirled before my eyes. We talked for a while, and he had all this flattering stuff to say, and I was getting a little uncomfortable. He said, "We all lived, I mean we *lived* to hear you say to one of us 'I think you're onto something there!'"

Michael

Michael:

The fact is, there are very few pats on the back in this profession. If we are going to think about "peace" in connection to composition and our classes, we should at least acknowledge a few moments where we may actually have made a difference. Otherwise, what happens to our faith in this process? I surely cannot say I have had such a positive influence on all of my students, Michael. What I do know, though, is that our students have the power to bring significant moments of peace to us.

Someone else. Karl Smith was an honors student in at least two years of high school classes with me. Karl, like many kids, sometimes acted goofy. I remember thinking that he was a bit immature. Once, an interdisciplinary Humanities class I taught was coming out of the school auditorium. I can't remember if we were listening to music and reading poetry or viewing art slides or what, but I remember yelling at Karl for cutting up or something. When he graduated from our school, some year or two later, he went to a local community college. One night he was riding his motorcycle, and he was struck and killed by a drunk driver. I went to the funeral home. I went out of a sense of responsibility to a family I didn't know well, but for whom I felt deeply—Karl was not their only child that I had taught. But there was Karl, in a blue suit with a white shirt whose neck seemed too big for him and with, as I recall, a wide old-fashioned tie. Many people I knew were there. It was a small town. So many students looking at me. Their eyes seemed to say, "Teacher, explain this."

About a week after the funeral, I was teaching a class when I got a call on the intercom, the principal wanted me to come to his office immediately. What, I wondered as I headed downstairs, was so important that I would be called to the principal's office during class? The principal met me outside the door to his office and escorted me in. Sitting there was Mr. and Mrs. Smith. They looked, as you might expect, exhausted. I thought, "Oh no! They are going to say 'Why did you yell at our son? Why were you so hard on him during his short time on earth?'" Of course I had been saying these things to myself for days since his death. Instead, Mr. Smith said, "We were going through Karl's things and found this piece of writing about you that he did for his entrance essay to college. He was supposed to write about someone who had influenced his life. We thought you might want it." The essay said something to the effect that my high school English teacher, Mr. Hurlbert, sometimes yells at me, and I deserve it because I act immature. I know, though, that Mr. Hurlbert cares, and I want to live up to his standards.

I can't explain all this incident means. Something terrible happened to that family—to Karl, yes, and to his parents and siblings. Still, they brought me Karl's words, and I am grateful for their generosity.

Mark

Mark:

Yes, it seems to me that Karl's words allow you to make some kind of peace with yourself. In this rare instance, someone—your student—has reached back to the living to offer a moment's peace. And you are right about the generosity of Karl's parents. They evidently recognized the power in their son's words.

There *is* power in their words, isn't there? I got a card at the end of last semester—a student had crossed out the "Merry Christmas" on the front and wrote "Happy Honika." Inside, he wrote,

> Dear Blitz,
>
> I was in your literature class in 1994. You probably don't even remember me, my name is Jeremy. I never said anything unless you were giving one of your famous oral quizzes (they made us all nervous, but they were kinda cool!). I got a C+ in your class so I wasn't one of your top notch students. Anyway, I got a job as a caseworker for the Youth Division, and I wanted to tell you that at my intake interview, I told them who had made the most serious impression on me in college—you! You probably never knew this, but I was always impressed when you would look at us at the beginning of every class and say "I'm glad you're here." At first it seemed weird—almost corny. But then I could tell you meant it, and after a while, I started to admire it. Remember that time you forgot to say it? That girl in the front said "aren't you gonna say your glad to

see us?" So you see you made a difference to me and so I want to wish you happy holidays and God bless you.

Your (former) student,
Jeremy

Michael

Michael:

Do you remember my telling you about Rabbi Miller? He lives on my street. He is in his eighties, a student of religion, physics, and philosophy. A Holocaust survivor. A gentle man.

Well, today I saw him for the first time in nearly a year. The first words he spoke to me were, "It's good to see you. It's still a complicated world and we still have much to do."

Mark

Birgit Brock-Utne writes, "An education for peace is an education for cooperation, for caring and sharing, for the use of non-violence in conflict-solving. An education that fosters competition, conquest, aggression and violence is an education for war" (72). Are we, as teachers, as parents, as a society, teaching the right things?

What are the right things? How do we get started? By realizing that peace is not a fancy suit we bring to our composition courses for students to try on for a couple of hours. If anything, we introduce a willingness to open up our classes, each time, to explorations of the ways things are and for imaginings of the ways things might be. With at least those two sources of motivation, we move with our students toward a design—and maybe at first it's not much more subtle than the crayon drawings given us by our children—for a moment of peace that will last long enough for us to feel it and learn something from it.

Our students come to our classes despite violence, in resistance to it, in search of answers for it, in the hopes of something other than it. Do they come for peace? We don't know. We honestly don't know what our students know about peace. The two of us grew up in the "Atomic Age." We were ducking and covering through primary school. We were shivering in the Cold War. We were watching friends and relatives fly off to

Vietnam to be shot by enemies and friendly fire. We were sitting at dinner tables with family members who were veterans of the Korean War, World War II, who had lost none of the America-love-it-or-leave-it bravado but who had lost the connections between what they'd supposedly fought for and what they could now actually claim to "have" and to "enjoy" back home.

But our students are growing up in a different age—a different war-consciousness. Their sense of war and peace is shaped as much by microviolences as by the Big War scenarios. What do they know of peace? They know it as a term in their history books; they know it as a chip of rhetoric, a sound bite in political speeches, a retro symbol of the '60s (which they now refer to as "back in the days"). And so if they come to us for peace, they come to us for the resolution of an image that is blurry, abstract, perhaps beyond them (perhaps beyond us). They do not, we'd guess, come expecting to have to *make* peace, and so when that is what we require (what we offer?), we can feel the disorientation, sometimes the resentment. What's this? Make peace? "Webster defines 'peace' as. . . ."

Mark:

I would like to consider a constructive/optimistic approach to our book. *Letters for the Living* should not be the occasion for a kind of hangdog 'sophisticated' despair. Rather, it should be a wake-up call, a spark of useful panic.

I'm thinking about Don Byrd's "Manifesto" where he writes:

> Culture is knowledge. What do people know? They know how to drive cars, operate computers, build buildings, televisions, nuclear weapons; they know how to live out the requirements of formal systems. If the engineers do manage to build people, they will build people who repeat the requirements of formal systems which produce them. They will not know why they do it. They will not know how to overcome their loneliness. They will not know how to read the world so they can act in their own best interest or in the best interest of their communities. They will not know how to teach the children to find meaning in their lives. They will have no way to assess what they have done for good or ill. They will not know why they whine. They will not know how to die (though ignorance will not stop them). ("Manifesto: Culture War" 2)

What do people know? What should they know? "Built" people may not know how to "read the world" nor to "teach the children to find meaning in their lives" nor to "overcome their loneliness," but all of us *can* know these things; or at least, we would argue, learning these things is central to the work of teachers and students, indeed to the work of being human.

Michael

Michael:

This afternoon Terry, Ro, and I arrived home in Pittsburgh from a New York trip to see family. Rabbi Miller saw us drive in and came up the street. We started talking, and he told me of a discussion group he had hosted at his house. The question on their agenda was God's nature. One of the participants asked the group how he was to understand God's mercy and justice when so many people in the world were still killing each other. To him, Rabbi Miller responded, "But look at how many people of the world live in peace."

Mark

Mark:

It's not likely that our students will live in peace if they cannot stand to be in their neighborhoods and homes. In *Future Dead Poets*, the poetry anthology[1] my students produced a few years back, one poet wrote:

> I hate this neighborhood.
>
> the junkies in the hall,
> the writing on the wall.
> the single pregnant teens,
> Be Boys in the corner looking mean
> car alarm going off at 3:00 a.m.
> I need some sleep
> in a few hours
> I have three final exams
>
> I hate the konyo carajo yelled at the kids next door.
> The sticky
> not yet dry urine
> on the building's entrance floor
>
> I hate
> to see the black and blues
> on Dona Therasa face
> I will pour gasoline
> down through these dirty stairs
> set this place on fire
> I'm sick and tired
> of so much hate
> in myself and in this place.

I want to think some more about homes and peace. In what sense can our students learn what they need so that they feel enabled to create homes where there is only housing, to create a *sense* of home where there is, now, only a sense of temporary warehousing (one of my students once wrote: "I live in a housing project that looks like it was put up for prisoners before they go to the Big House—except we're not going anywhere.").

What about home? In the larger sense, we have wondered about the connections and disconnections between literacy education and a better community—a better world. When we get to know our students, we learn, again and again, that they carry their families with them—their children, their parents, their brothers and sisters. Many of my students have left their families "back home" in another country: Haiti, the Dominican Republic, Salvador, Peru, Russia, China, Korea, Guyana, Jamaica, Barbados, India, Pakistan, Egypt, Nigeria, and South Africa. Many of your graduate students have come from as far away as Togo, Saudi Arabia, Burundi, Venezuela, Iraq, and Jordan. Our students *miss* their families. They keep their families and their homelands in their daily consciousness. We also need to think about the more immediate departures our students make every day. After the day's work at college, they head home (or off to work and then home) to what? In some cases, their homes are truly oases in the midst of deserts of literal and figurative kinds. But in other cases, they return to living conditions that drain the life right out of them. Their sense of home becomes dislocated—perhaps they find home in another person, a lover, a baby. If "home is where the heart is," and if the heart aches for love and safety, one makes a home with angels on the head of a pin.

Mark, my students see so many buildings going up (and down) and, at the same time, see so little improvement in their actual communities, their projects, their buildings, their sense of home. What can this do to their sense of being in the larger society? And what do you and I know of such things? We know something, it's true, but we need to learn much, much more from the people we teach and who are right there, in the exactly proper position to teach us things so important that to ignore them is to commit an act of cruelty.

Michael

Michael:

I think the concept of home is important for another reason, too. If we and our students can learn ways to tune ourselves to, to record and examine the ways we act in—or survive—our homes, we have a significant opportunity to make some important articulations about where we come from, but maybe most important, who we are and want to become.

So many of my students have written powerful books about violent homes, dangerous homes, homes filled with pain. And of surviving these homes. One student wrote of her stepfather: "This was the way things always were. Every night he came home drunk, the walls in our house would shake with the shouting." She then recounts his arrest for DWI and his subsequent process of recovery from alcoholism.

Another student wrote a book which begins in the first days of a semester and a phone call from her mother who had just discovered her husband's latest affair and had decided to divorce him. The student takes her readers through the day of the phone call, of walking through a college book store, "crowded with what seems to be a million college students all pushing, shoving, and bitching over the same things. No one says 'thank you,' 'excuse me,' or 'I'm sorry.' Nobody is aware or seems to care if you had a bad morning. It's the last thing on their minds, but it's the first on yours." Through her new fears, "As for me, tuition takes on a whole new meaning. I do have my mom, but it's going to be tough for her too. She will have bills, rent, and then there's groceries, gas for the car, medical bills, and much more. How could I ask her to help me pay for college? I refuse to give my mother more to worry about." The student ends her book by recounting her mother's bravery, sacrifices, and strength of character, something the daughter has, I would add, no doubt inherited.

Of course, the majority of my students return to homes far different from your students, as we already know, as the majority of mine live in dorms and fraternity and sorority houses (though I teach a fair number of off-campus and "non-traditional students" and family people, too).

What can they teach us?
matters
turning on darkness
and carving space
out of rooms
short of breath
long in pain
short of time

Michael, I was recently reading a realistic, though hopeful, poem by Paul Hoover. In "South of X," Hoover writes about violence (particularly Vietnam) and hope in the latter half of our century:

> Something huge and
> warm within the
> room and you.

> We leaned and
> stared at it.
> Thus perceptions of

> design meet with
> final cause to
> mean a thing

> is real. Nothing
> real is fast. (83)

Sometimes something real (a home?), despite hopeful love, is not possible. The violence swirls around us: we hurt each other; we hurt ourselves; we are beaten up and we deliver beatings. Not all the students who write about troubled homes find hopeful endings, but many do.

Through it all we try to climb out of it—some of us by writing:

> Wretched and amazed,
> love allows such
> nights on the
> roofs of all
> creation. (Hoover 85–86)

I think that, taken together as something of a whole, the writing our students and we are trying to do is a chronicle of such nights, a chronicle of our attempts to make these kinds of nights (homes) more readily accessible. This chronicle is a powerful testament to hope in a troubled and tired time. It's just that these nights are so filled with contradictory meanings, so many of these nights short-lived.

Mark

_____

Mark:

When I was young and my sisters and I were visiting with my father, he insisted we call his apartment(s) "home," and we tried, but it always seemed artificial.

I have been worried about how my own children would deal with their two "homes" and made a point of never arguing one way or the other for how they should regard either place, either parent. I've just loved them as hard as I can, and have provided as safe and cozy and homey a place for them in this undersized apartment as I can. They, themselves, have come to call it their home. They seem completely comfortable with the idea that they have two *homes*, and that each is *theirs,* with their things, their signs, their marks.

Mark, you wrote:

What can they teach us?
matters
turning on darkness
and carving space
out of rooms
short of breath
long in pain
short of time

Mark—I want to be sure to say, even after all these years of writing together, of sharing our lives, trials, pains and joys, I still consider these bits of poetry the best kind of gift-giving.

What, precisely, do we find unacceptable in our teaching? That there *are* limits to achieving a safe, fulfilling life? (Of course there are.) That there are limits to what any one—or one thousand—teachers can do toward opening a way for students to remake, change, understand, dwell comfortably in their homes and lives? Of course there are. That there are limits that are literally sprung up out of these acts of composition? That in the act and process of writing, our students risk opening themselves up to the kinds of distress that Jim Berlin worried so much about in the *Composition and Resistance* roundtables? As he would say again and again, it's *not* the "good life" (137) toward which we are pointing anyone. It's merely "the life," such as it is, such as it may be when our students dwell within it prepared with the meager few, new instruments they may learn to play while they are with us.

Michael

_____

Michael:

The fact that we are comfortable breaking the prose of letters to make the language do what we want it to do at a given moment—to serve a need, to answer something—is certainly one of the greatest gifts of our friendship. Perhaps it is a desire to share this bit of luxury that motivates me to encourage my students to break form and genre in their own work.

Terry, Ro, and I went to upstate New York for Christmas. Seeing family was good, but I felt like the Christmas cur at the table. Being in Fulton County and the small mill town where I grew up is sometimes so strange and depressing. As the leather workers were leaving for the holiday weekend, some were told not to come back as two mills were closing. One mill employed 475 men and women. The men there were also told that their pension fund was bankrupt. One 57-year-old man told my brother (this is the mill he quit a few years back after many years there) that he didn't know what he would do: 57, no retirement, a family, and nowhere to work. Another mill closed, and the executives of the mill each got a two hundred thousand dollar severance bonus. The men got something like two weeks.

Two guys who claim to be socialists or Marxists or something have a slot on the local TV cable access station. It's a call-in show. They spend their time complaining that the rich mill owners should not be allowed to get rich off the backs of the workers, that all profits should be shared. They sound sincere and angry—and passé—all at once. Many cranks call in to bait them or for the thrill of calling them "assholes" on TV, but occasionally an angry union agitator calls in to agree and spur on the anger—though what good comes of it I don't know—faith, belief, momentary hope? I heard a woman call in to talk about how she was mistreated in the mills and how her husband is among the walking dead because of the mills. It's so sad and hopeless.

Michael, there are sections of Gloversville and Johnstown where the houses are literally falling apart. The downtown "four corners" is filled with the out of work. These streets always look the same; the people look the same as every other time I've been back "home."

Christmas day—driving through a mill neighborhood. Two people in worn
clothes. A young woman walking—a young man, her boyfriend?, two steps
behind her, stooped, carrying three bags of groceries. They aren't speaking.
She walks quickly—staring straight ahead. He does not look up from the
sidewalk. I feel something, sadness, fear, and maybe relief that I'm not them—
though I was once close—and anger at myself for thinking these thoughts.

Mark

Mark:

Our students do remarkable things when they feel sure they can do remarkable things. If I can do nothing else, I want them to feel, to *know,* they can.

Here's why I'm telling you this. There's a guy in my Freshman Composition
class who simply cannot stand having to write anything. He tries. His weekly
journal has the requisite 5 pages of writing in it. He's tried all the things that
other students do to fulfill this portion of the course: taken walks around the
block, around his neighborhood, gone for "ethnographic" rides on trains and
busses, even interviewed family members about his own personal history.
Still, his journal writings are so utterly devoid of enthusiasm, of energy, it
makes me feel bad about making him do this thing.

As you know, in my class, every day, five or six students read aloud from a
portion of their journals. And once each week, students work in small groups
to read each other's journals and to write a couple of pages of response to
some thing(s) they find there. Earlier in the week, the young man I mentioned
above looked particularly morose as the notebook exchange began. His group
for the day had six members. For the next half hour, students were busy
reading, smiling, frowning, puzzling, questioning, and writing up a storm.
Occasionally I was invited to one group or another to have a look at something someone wrote.

Yesterday, I collected a batch of journals and discovered, in that young man's
book, a kind of poem. I can't be sure he meant it to be a poem, but I also
couldn't help reading it as one. I won't quote it all here, but part of it went:

> My mom looked so tired today,
> My dad did, too. So did I when I went to brush my teeth.
> We all looked tired and it's only the morning.
> What will the rest of the day be like?

Mark, remarkable thing number one is that this piece of writing so obviously
meant something for him. Rather than lacking energy, it cut to the heart of a
weariness. It takes a great deal of energy to portray life so clearly. The rest of
the poem was about how hard people in his family have always had to work
because, as he put it, "We're not the smartest or the toughest family around."
But remarkable thing number two was what his classmates wrote back to him.
Up to that entry, as bland as his writings had been, so had been most of the

responses. But this time, everyone in his group tried to write something encouraging, something enthusiastic. They were obviously cheering him on. I should add that I have not been aware that anyone in the class had ever paid much attention to him. And yet here were five responses to his writing, to his thinking, that were meant to draw him out, and to draw him into a kind of community.

Michael

_____

Michael:

I received a letter from Jim Sledd. Here's a quote that seems, somehow, related to that story about your student's journal: "Though the role of the Dutch boy at the leaky dike quickly becomes absurd, I try to remember son Andrew's injunction: 'Everyone reach one.'"

Look what your student has done. Sometimes one can reach many. So, yes, sometimes our students will do remarkable things. But I believe this only happens when their teachers believe they will; when their teachers know something remarkable is about to happen; when their teachers haven't learned to stop looking for the remarkable, to stop hearing it when it happens, to stop thinking. It has something to do with knowing poetry when you find it. Is everything our students write poetry? Is everything remarkable? I don't think so. But enough is to keep the search for it alive.

Mark

_____

Mark:

Just got back from a poetry reading I did at Biblio's in Manhattan. It went well—a full house (about half a dozen colleagues, 15 students or so, a few friends, and another two dozen or so that I didn't know—all told, maybe 50 or 60 people in a small cafe). Mark, I'll tell you, I was startled by how many people came up to talk about the poetry, often about particular pieces, or to buy a book because they'd heard something from it and wanted a bunch of it. Amazing. More astounding was the fact that so many students came. I was delighted to see them.

I also did a very different kind of reading the other night. It was at this year's AIDS Awareness Dinner, the closing ceremony to a week of AIDS Awareness events around New York City and, in particular, CUNY. The woman who organized the event had come to a poetry reading I'd done last year; she contacted me a few months ago and told me she'd been moved by some of my work. She asked me to write a poem for the AIDS Awareness closing night, and I told her I would be honored to do so. What made the event so memorable was that the whole evening was an occasion where people had come together from the university community, the outside community, some of our faculty and students, and dozens of people who had lost loved ones to AIDS and were participating in the ceremonies as a way of finding a little peace for themselves. Here's the poem I wrote (and read):

Poem for AIDS Awareness Week, 1996

This is a photograph of Charles and Little Charles. The mysterious
illness that made the year 1978 the last of Little Charles' life,
took Big Charles in 1980.
This is a picture of Jim in 1977.
The proverbial big-guy,
ham-handed, ROTC, All-American,
13 years later, Jim was dying,
thinner than the laughter
around his hospital bed
when he had joked,
"you'd have to be stupid
to sleep with anyone anymore."
Here is Angela—gone for two years now,
her mother, Gloria, alive but also HIV+
cursing a god who would make her outlive her daughter.
This is Sherise, whose new husband's
previously unknown
sexual history
did her in this past March;
This is Eugene, diagnosed with hemophilia in 1979 and with AIDS in
1988;
Here's a before-shot of Richard at 23 playing hockey and an after-shot
of Richard 21 months later, looking 100 years old with less than 48
hours to live.
Here's a picture of someone's face
waiting out the Elisa test-results—
negative means you live to whisper
in an ad-magazine ear "I'm negative."—and positive means a follow-up
test, to confirm, to seal your place
in this remembering.
Here's a slide-show of people with AIDS and without homes,
Here's a 1985 group-photo of me, my ex-wife, and 6 of her medical
school classmates at a black-tie dinner, listening to the keynote speaker
say,
"AIDS is not a plague. You watch.
In ten years, it will be as curable as Tonsillitis."
This is a photo-exhibit of children with AIDS, an anthology of writings by
people
with loved ones who have died of AIDS,
a newspaper photograph of an entire family with AIDS, a public service
television spot featuring a famous person with AIDS,
There's Tom Hanks as Andrew Beckett in *Philadelphia,*
playing a lawyer with AIDS,

trying to find a lawyer
who won't run from AIDS,
and there's Andrew Beckett, dying from AIDS, filling up theater after
theater with people who cry, refreshed by a couple of hours of cinematic
grief, comforted by Andrew's sanitized, peaceful death, surrounded by
loved ones,
affairs in order,
lover standing by to carry the torch.
There's nothing peaceful or orderly
or sanitized about AIDS.
Here is a CNN camera shot of
of a congressional subcommittee
slowly awakening from the slumber
of a velvety soft stupidity,
stepping all over each other to say something important about "this
terrible menace"—
Susan Sontag said
that when you see illness as a monster,
you end up fighting it as though you are a cartoon character. AIDS is no
monster,
and we
are not cartoons.
Our friends and lovers,
brothers and sisters,
parents and children,
husbands and wives
don't live frame-by-frame inside color animation, able to rise each time
their bodies
are blown to bits.
This is a video tape of someone
you will not be able to know,
he cannot smile for the camera;
she cannot pretend to be in a Hallmark moment, he cannot stop
throwing up,
she is nearly comatose from fever and pain, he cannot afford the
hospitalization,
she doesn't have the energy to reach the clinic nor the money
for treatment of Pneumocystitis.
One year later, that same medication can be gotten, experimentally,
for free.
This man has gone for months without seeing a loved one because he
wants to spare them the sight of a body ravaged by Caposi's Sar-
coma—
in this video tape everyone is saying their last good-byes. There is
nothing poignant about AIDS,
nor about the deepening community of mourners. We don't mourn to
become part of an eloquent sound-byte, we don't cry at the beauty of an
enormous, traveling quilt—we cry because the AIDS quilt
is enormous,
because we can feel the stifling heat of it creeping up our legs,
because each and every intricate panel is whip-stitched into our
consciousness,

because we now can calculate
that more than one-third of the people
in this room
will know someone, already know someone, or will be someone
to die of AIDS.
This is a strip of pictures from a Penn station photo-booth. Thomas and
his sister, Diane—
1991 he tested positive—not for HIV, but for cancer, 1992 he had no
immunity,
1993 the chemo wasn't working,
the acupuncture wasn't working,
the herbal medicines and meditation,
the prayers, the friends, the Leukovorin rescue, the tears of his sister
weren't working,
1994 we all met for Thomas' funeral—
crying, consoling, shaking our heads.
I heard Diane say, a dozen times,
"No, it wasn't AIDS,
it wasn't AIDS,
it was cancer."
And it was true.
It wasn't AIDS.
But it was so hard to fathom
a young man's death without AIDS.
Can we have absorbed the anxiety of an illness so completely that we
cannot imagine dying without it? This is a picture of you and me.
Alive in a time when we have come to spell Death A.I.D.S.—
A time when time stops
with every diagnosis of HIV+,
A time when fewer and fewer of us can say "It wasn't AIDS,
it wasn't AIDS."
This is a picture in which more and more of the people are disappear-
ing,
this is an entire photograph album not of living memories but of
suffering we will have to die to forget. This is a library full of stories
not about AIDS, not about monsters,
but about people,
people with AIDS,
and those who take care of people with AIDS, people afraid of contracting AIDS, and
people who ought to be more afraid of contracting AIDS, people working
to cure AIDS, and
people desperate to be cured of AIDS,
people who spread AIDS,
people who have grown up equating sex, and blood transfusions, with
AIDS, people who devote their lives to helping those with AIDS, people
who refuse to acknowledge the reality of AIDS, and people who get in
the way of those working to end AIDS. This is an archive of stories and
pictures and words and money
and time
and running out of time
and running toward a time

when we will say the words
Acquired Immune Deficiency Syndrome
and not mean Death.
This is a photograph someone should take of a gathering like this one, sometime
maybe in our lifetimes,
if you look closely you may see, in our expressions, the clear gazes of people for whom
sharing an oversized quilt might once again mean only that the winter
nights are cold and that we have learned, once more,
how to keep each other warm and safe
and alive.

Mark, just writing, and then reading this poem, made me think about those that I have known who have died, and I've been thinking that writing poetry has always been at the core of what I do to make sense of living, to make peace. Yes, poetry also causes, and reflects, sorrows and trials, but, for me, there could be no peace for myself if not for writing at the heart of how I live. It takes occasions like these for me to allow myself to remember I do this work, too.

Now I'm going to crash. Daina lost her first tooth. When she called to tell me, she sounded so proud.

Michael

———————————

Michael:

Your poem is remarkable. Thank you. I want to say more, and I also want to say nothing. Just as I tell my students that silences may be filled with appreciation, with pleasure, I tell you the same.

How is it that you and I are ever able to lose sight of the possibilities of poetry and poetics in our lives as teachers of composing? Look how your reading created a space where students could be members of an audience at a cafe reading (and knowing what I know of your students' lives, I guess this was something new for them to be). We have said again and again to each other that our lives as teachers are not disconnected from our lives as writers, husband(s), fathers, friends, writers, lovers of art and music, any more than our students' lives and loves are disconnected from their work. And no part of our lives can be understood in disconnection to the other. Tonight at Biblio's your life as a poet made something possible for your students—and don't forget, while we are at it, what your students taught you tonight about the teacher you are and about the power of poetry to resituate people, at least for the moment. And this goes double for the AIDS Awareness reading from the other night. Don't forget these things, Michael.

Here's something written by one of my colleagues:

Poetry appears to be the unfinished business of the race as well as the poet. To talk about this means inevitably to talk about damage and mending, wounding and healing. (Rosaly DeMaios Roffman 527)

Congratulations on the readings.

Mark

Mark:

In the 55 seconds I have before I go to teach, one thing we are finding out is what, if anything, is on the other side of complaint. I don't mean (only) whining. I mean the sort of large-scale, hyper-critical, sometimes-cynical, often-mistaken-for-knowledge-itself complaining that Robert Hughes discusses in *Culture of Complaint,* the kind of complaints our culture constructs as ENDgames, not (as I'm beginning to realize) as engines of change. Or rather they are fuel, a potential that becomes corrosive when it is not used, or at the very least, a very heavy load of debris.

One can read the opening 20 pages of *Beloved* and rediscover a vision of magic that is both restorative and terrible in its implications—so rare, so rare— ours is a horribly dulled culture, the fineness, the freshness, the alertness is vanishing.

Michael

Michael:

What an experience. It is midnight. I just read a book by one of my under- graduate writing students. She wrote about her search for what she calls the "magic" of her life and home, her quest to determine how her rural Western PA life is not just "common," "typical, mundane." The book is about growing up in rural Pennsylvania with her extended family living in the nearby houses. And it contains some remarkably clear memories from childhood, of seeing, for instance, her grandparents working in their garden, of playing in the attic of their house with her cousins.

By the end of her book, this student discovers it; she can put a name to the magic that surrounds her. She writes so beautifully that her words are with me now, even though I have put the book down and turned to e-mail you: "I now realize that I am not average. I am loved." So simply, so directly this young woman tells such a truth about her life and family. A truth which I need to find ways of remembering in my own life—every day.

Mark

Mark:

I want to post the following note from one of my students. She was a student of mine years ago in a technical writing course. She is enormously bright and well-read, cheerful and clever. Now she is in my poetry course, delighted to be there (as I am to see her again), but also, as ever, smartly critical of all sorts of things. In her journal, she keeps records of her readings, ideas, poems about her African heritage, course-related troubles, and so on. She wrote the following:

> Thought for the day: I know poetry is not a whitefolk/blackfolk thing, but how come all the poems by blacks only speak about how hard life is? Do we live on the same planet, or what? Professor, aren't there pretty poems by Black people? Of course there are, but we'll never see them in school. No, we'll only read poems like "The Weary Blues" (Hughes) or "If We Must Die" (McKay). I want pretty, Professor, pretty!

> The sun is shining
> The leaves are green
> The flowers are blooming
> The birds are singing
> The children are playing
> And the world is just
> Fucking wonderful!

Mark, I think about a passage from *The Philosophy of Peace* (Somerville): "Real education is, of course, a great spiritual challenge to habitual prejudices and merely conventional patterns" (257). My student, above, wants a real education and knows how to ask for it, to contribute to it.

Michael

———————————

Mark:

It's been raining here for two days; there's something very soothing about steady rain that promises to let up shortly after the reservoirs are topped off. At night, when I can't sleep, I sit with my feet up on the window sill, maybe sipping a scotch, looking at the rain and the street, and when I think about how many times and in how many places you and I have sat with our feet up on the window ledge, looking out into one night or the other, sipping a scotch or a beer and feeling that at least there is this important connection to someone else in the world; when I can focus on this, I am aware of at least one good reason to persist.

Yours in our persistences,

Michael

———————————

Mark:

One semester, in the course of a discussion I've now forgotten, a student asked me, "Do you like all of us?" The class first looked at her—surprised, but also delighted. Then, in the big horseshoe of a configuration we were in, all eyes turned to me. I remember smiling—also delighted—almost with a sinister glee, which tickled them all the more. I said "No." There was abrupt laughter—relief that I'd: (1) answered quickly; (2) answered in a way that would not automatically set off the bullshit-detector. And then there was crazy curiosity. "Who?" she wanted to know—now that she was silently elected spokesperson. "Yeah, who?" a few more demanded. Smiles all around—expectant—a few were not smiling. I tried not smiling. "Now, I can't tell you that." Nervous silence. We went on with whatever we were doing. Lots of cooperation, fewer smiles and quieter tones. Toward the end of class, one student pointed out how everything felt different now. I agreed. I also pointed out that one of the luxuries of getting to know people over a semester is that even someone we start out disliking we can get to like. Someone said that this also meant that someone we liked we could end up disliking. "Yup," I said. So now what do we do, we all wondered. Someone proposed—and I could have hugged him—that it wouldn't be a bad idea to find a way to like each other so we didn't have to feel uncomfortable all semester. The small groups worked very well thereafter, no incidents, much cooperation, and a few apparently strong friendships—pretty much like any workshop class—but maybe this one had a worthwhile edge to it.

Michael

Michael:

I don't know as I've heard of many classroom moments more honest than that one. The amazing thing is that it didn't crumble in your hands. That was nearly China Syndrome, my friend. Your class, if it had taken one wrong turn, might have melted down. The other amazing thing is that out of such honesty came such a positive reaction instead of hard feelings. When I picture that group of students, I am particularly impressed by their ability to overcome "New York defensive living." It's also interesting to me that it was a student who "saved" the day without the use of "control rods!"

Today was one of those great days when it all worked. My students' energies were high. They seemed in good spirits. We all felt glad to be working together. When we left the room(s), there was a sense that something important was going on and we were a part of it.

On days like this, when I think about how many of these same students still have problems as draining as ever, and when I recall what so many of them must go home to, I appreciate even more what they must have called upon to make a day like this happen for themselves.

On Sunday, Roland, Terry, and I went to see the Pirates. Between innings, I took Ro to a stand and bought him an ice cream cone. On the way back to our seat, he got tired so I carried him. At one point he looked at his ice cream cone—then at me—he smiled—there was such love and pride and pleasure in his face, I almost cried.

Mark

Mark:

It's 7 AM. I have been up since 5:30 when Cory padded over to my bed and climbed in to snuggle. Daina stirred at 6, climbed down from her "loft" and joined us as well. I miss such moments on a more regular basis, but I am grateful for all of them when they happen. Now, after a rousing breakfast of Froot Loops, they're building with blocks, gluing ice-cream sticks to paper towel tubes, arguing over who's been knocking whose block tower down, and humming camp tunes. I live for mornings like this.

Michael

Michael:

When I was a kid and was attending church, I remember the masses (ended, I think) with the priest saying something like, "Peace be with you." To which the congregation responded, "And also with you." I may be far away from the religious experience, but I don't want to be far from that sentiment.

Mark

We cannot educate for peace, we *cannot*, if we lose our abilities to appreciate, to be moved, by those moments in which we are well. We cannot ask our students to envision a better world if we don't know what touches us when we glimpse even an instant of such a world. It is difficult to know how much of the personal to bring to bear on what we do as educators, but it would be a mistake to bring none of it. With what instruments can we educate for peace? "Light and dreams in the palm of the hand?" Can we imagine *better* teaching tools?

> . . . elementary school children are provided opportunities to plant seeds and take care of plants in their classrooms. Children bring

bouquets to their teachers, and some schools encourage their students to sell seeds as part of their contribution to school improvement projects. It is almost as if elementary school children were being prepared for something of great importance, but high school rejects the core of existential studies and concentrates on the periphery—on the skills and incidental information gathered during exploration. An opportunity to study response, beauty, and almost mystical interdependence is lost. (Noddings 132)

While there are many fine and courageous high school teachers out there, we know that Noddings is, in general, right about the weakness of high school curricula. And college is equally bad. Not nearly enough has changed since 1969 when Norman Soloman and his fellow high school students in the Montgomery County Student Alliance wrote,

The school system takes young people who are interested in the things around them and destroys this natural joy in discovering and learning. Genuine, honest reasons for wanting to learn are quashed and replaced with an immediate set of rewards (which educators say are not ends in themselves but which nevertheless become just that). (Montgomery County Student Alliance 149)

What happened to those seeds? We need to develop a philosophical frame of mind where we believe that every student is "being prepared for something of great importance." We need to create curricula which include ample "opportunity to study response, beauty, and almost mystical interdependence."

Michael:

I had one of the best sessions of my graduate course, Rhetorical Traditions, tonight. The class had read excerpts from *The Koran* and *The Talmud*, along with articles about teaching students of Arab descent and an essay by Martin Buber about the possibility of dialogue even in the face of great obstacles. After much discussion, a graduate student from Jordan, Leah, attempted to articulate the ways in which the rhythms of *The Koran* are always in her head, a beautiful and honored inheritance, even as she writes in English. She then chanted a section of *The Koran* for us, in the classic style. We talked about the rhythms of sacred texts and how these rhythms imbue the composing processes of each of us with something uniquely ours. Elliot, an American Jew, then chanted a Hebrew prayer he remembered from the time of his youth. Something in the conflation of their two voices, of their willingness to risk sharing things so deeply personal with each other and the rest of the class, something in this meeting of the spiritual and the academic was very—moving certainly—but more than that—restorative. There was reverence for each other among the students, despite the dramatic differences in nationality and ethnicity. My hope, indeed, the challenge, is to encourage these teachers of composition to take such impulses toward health into their own classrooms.

A Puerto Rican student, Jorge, recently said about Rhetorical Traditions, "There is a difference between classes you take and classes you live."

Mark

Mark:

Yes, again and again . . . our students are alive.
They are alive despite threads of death and
sadness and suffering whip-stitched along
the seams between them,
and between them and us, an entire
alphabet of potential misunderstanding
and deafness . . . and yet
we listen and we learn something,
and they know we are listening
because they know what it means to listen
because they have been listening all along,
and along the lines we fix our lives to,
we live because we are alive when we are alive together.

Michael

Michael:

In a section of Humanities Literature, the students decided that for their whole-class collective project, they wanted to write a book of their own, a diary. They wanted, as they put it, to create a work of contemporary literature that portrayed their lives as truthfully as they possibly could (and of course, I asked them to write and include a reflective reading of the book). I also suggested, and they agreed, that all of their entries be published anonymously, to protect their privacy. In fact, I even designed an elaborate scheme whereby they could give each other suggestions for revising their entries for the class diary without revealing their identities even to each other.[2]

As I now read the book, *Blue*, I am struck by its honesty. My students tell the reality of their lives. And what is the reality? Many of my students know love and health in their families. Many of them suffer self-inflicted violence, such as alcohol abuse. Too many of them seem unable to find value in the love relations they have at the same time that they seem to desire love so badly. And too many of them live in fear for their lives—one student, for instance, was being tested, during the semester, for a life-threatening form of cancer—

something she never told me or the other students. *Blue* is a book about enduring, Michael, sometimes well and sometimes not so well. The fact that these students survive the days and nights detailed in *Blue*, the fact that they even make such a book, carry full loads of classes, and sometimes hold down jobs, is a testament to their heart.

Here is the last entry in the diary:

> Things got to me today. I miss Jen, a lot. I realized I have no real friends because I have been so comfortable with Jen for over a year. Now she is gone, and I am left alone to face the fuck face in the mirror. Sometimes, like today, I hate myself. I hate the fact that I am an addict, I got a record, I'm a felon, I broke up with my girl, and all the pain I feel ain't going away anytime soon. So I'm feeling all this shit, yeah get out the violins and pity my sorry ass, god I am sick! Oh yeah, I'm jonesin' for junk, too. I want to say fuck life. And then I picked up my mom's 9mm, choose a bullet, and decide maybe I'll try the suicide thing for the hundredth time. I sat there on my bed with a clip loaded in one hand and a pistol in the other. I called my ex-girlfriend, did the self pity thing.
> Then I said to myself, "Why man, why?" So I'm in pain, I got a few sick problems, but man, I can deal and I got a choice. I didn't get clean and get off of drugs to be miserable, so why am I doing this to myself?" I hung the phone up and put the gun away, then I went to a meeting.

Michael, this student and I have talked about life, about growing up in small towns, and about fathers. He later wrote to me, as part of his evaluation of *Blue*:

> I believe it does offer hope, because of the last entry. I wrote it so I know. The last line, "I went to a meeting," may not seem so profound to anyone else. I'm going to tell you that that fucking meeting saved my life. I would not be sitting here, writing this if I hadn't gone. That sounds like hope to me—sick, twisted, and distorted—but it's hope.

It is hope, Michael. I don't presume to say that my class was anywhere near as important to my student as that meeting was, but I know that it counts. He has told me things that matter. In fact, the things he says and writes matter so much that I cannot help but wonder by what mechanisms—school or otherwise—he would be taught to think that a line like "I went to a meeting" is anything less than profound.

Mark

Notes

1. In Michael's poetry workshops, students have produced various collective projects ranging from anthologies like *Future Dead Poets* to one class's poetry performance video. The anthologies are edited by the entire class, so the work contained in them is produced with the intention and knowledge that the

work will be printed and distributed widely throughout the college and to people outside the college. These anthologies are printed in editions of 100 to 200 copies and are distributed to the John Jay College faculty, the library, the administration and, if students request it, to family members.

2. Mark was able to keep students' identities a secret during the making of *Blue* by developing elaborate mechanisms of class management. On days when students would workshop each other's writing, Mark would have all forty-five students lay their unsigned drafts out on the floor in a secured hallway outside the room, then each student would go out, one at a time, and pick a draft at random to bring back to the room for the reading and response. At the end of this activity, the students put all the materials back out in the hall. Then, one at a time, the writers would go out into the hall and pick up their work, unseen by the rest of the class.

Introduction to Part 4

Mark:

You and I aren't going to change the world, and to say that worries me. I often feel big pieces of idealism slipping away. On the other hand, I do think you and I are involved in the alchemy of making as many good things possible for groups of people who have come to us, specifically, for a reminder of what human beings might do when they are permitted to think as a legitimate activity, when they are encouraged to dream and to invent, when they are celebrated for sometimes a single step that for them is as good as the most gigantic leap of faith. It beats a step off the edge into the abyss.

There's no time for anything except right now and a strong push for a bit later. That's what I am doing with my students and with my kids and—I wish more often—and in better style—with myself: making as strong a push as I can for moving the "right now" into a possibility of "a little later."

Michael

_____

Michael:

Right now my idealism would be doing its swan dive but I am listening and screaming to The Neighborhoods:

> Hate zone, I don't want to live in this
> Hate zone, . . .

Mark

4 Letters

We want to be able to walk away from this book with the idea that educating for peace works. We want to be able to "close" by saying that peace follows violence just as our "Peace" section comes after "Violence." But this section, "Letters," is really a re-opening. The wounds are open, the eyes are open, the possibilities are open, and the mouths are open, trying to say things to us, from us, that we have barely begun to learn how to hear, to allow ourselves to say. It took a *New York Times* television commercial to remind America that the word *listen* is also the word *silent*—each turned inside out and around the other. In "Letters," we should fade out the sound, we should shut off the lights, we should tie up the threads, and we should dead-bolt, chain, and gate the store. Instead, there is so much more to say, more to examine under the lights, threads that must dangle awhile, and a bunch of open doors through which we invite anyone who wants to keep unscrambling the "letters for the living" so that we can spell and say and live the words and actions that will truly change the world.

You want to know about grading papers, about whether we teach grammar, about how many sections we teach, about how many students are in our classes, about release time, about committee work, about whether we spend enough time in the classroom to appreciate how difficult and time-consuming and nearly impossible it is to keep up with the planning, reading, and evaluating and discussing, not to mention research and writing we might want to do. We'll cut to the chase. Of course we read lots of student papers. Of course we write marginal notes that sometimes include reminders to watch out for one or another kind of grammatical problem. We write comments in praise of, and critical of, student essays, letters, paragraphs, research papers, theses, and dissertations. Our writing classes mostly have between twenty-five and forty students in them; each of our course loads is around eight courses per year. In a given year, Mark reads and/or directs dissertations and gives comprehensive doctoral exams; Michael and Mark supervise independent studies, Michael also supervises at least fifteen interns working at local public service agencies, we both teach summer courses, and both of us serve on altogether too many committees and task forces. We are first and foremost classroom teachers. That's what this book is about: what happens in our classes.

What *does* happen in our classes? Students write, we write, we all talk, we read and write some more. We would guess that you do much the same, and no doubt your stories and your students' stories could fill books of your own.

We cannot say enough about the people whose everyday lives touch our lives so profoundly. And that's the point. Where are the stories of the real lives of those we teach, of those whose writings fill our days and, often, our nights? Where are these books?

They're out there.

Many books on literacy education include narratives about and by real students, many and deep examples of students' writings and voices, actual teachers' narratives and correspondence, and all toward ideas for creating better places in which to live. We have in mind the depiction of the lives of teachers and students in David Schaafsma's *Eating on the Street: Teaching Literacy in a Multicultural Society*; the accounts of the lives of students from home as well as school in Danling Fu's *"My Trouble Is My English": Asian Students and the American Dream*; the artful presentation and theorizing of student conversation in Mary Ann Cain's *Revisioning Writers' Talk: Gender and Culture in Acts of Composing*; the representations of the students' school experiences in Harriet Malinowitz's *Textual Orientations: Lesbian and Gay Students and the Making of Discourse Communities*; the graduate students' narratives in Sandra Hollingsworth's *Teacher Research and Urban Literacy Education: Lessons and Conversations in a Feminist Key*; Jonathan Kozol's powerful study, *Savage Inequalities: Children in America's Public Schools*; the revealing narrative of Victor Villanueva's *Bootstraps: From an American Academic of Color*; and the inclusion of student experience at the center of Gail Tayko and John Tassoni's *Sharing Pedagogies: Students and Teachers Write about Dialogic Practices*. Similarly, we have in mind David Downing's *Changing Classroom Practices: Resources for Literary and Cultural Studies*. And this is only a start.

There are also the other books that help us understand our teaching. Arguing the value of writing that encourages imagination, craft, and the intellectual rigor of subjectivity, Scott Russell Sanders claims that writing about one's family and home is a way of making "a meaningful gathered life in a world that seems broken and scattered" (ix). In *The University in Ruins*, Bill Readings writes about what it means to be a teacher at this time in history. He proposes that, within the academy, we find new ways of forming communities, groups constructed around particular, affirmative projects. In *Other People's Children: Cultural Conflict in the Classroom,* Lisa Delpit challenges us to consider some tough questions that seem to us to be precisely the right ones to ask:

> We all carry worlds in our heads, and those worlds are decidedly different. We educators set out to teach, but how can we reach the worlds of others when we don't even know they exist? Indeed, many of us don't even realize that our own worlds exist only in our heads and in the cultural institutions we have built to support them. It is as if we are in the middle of a great computer-generated virtual reality game, but the "realities" displayed in various participants' minds are entirely different terrains. When one player moves right and up a hill, the other player perceives him as moving left and into a river.
>
> What are we really doing to better educate poor children and children of color? Sporadically we hear of "minorities" scoring higher in basic skills, but on the same newspaper page we're informed of their dismal showing in higher-order thinking skills. We hear of the occasional school exemplifying urban excellence, but we are inundated with stories of inner-city mass failure, student violence, and soaring drop-out rates. We are heartened by new attempts at school improvement—better teacher education, higher standards, revised curricula—even while teachers of color are disappearing from the workforce and fiscal cutbacks increase class sizes, decimate critical instructional programs, and make it impossible to repair the buildings that are literally falling down around our children's heads.
>
> What should we be doing? The answers, I believe, lie not in a proliferation of new reform programs but in some basic understandings of who we are and how connected and disconnected we are from one another. (xiv–xv)

So, yes, the stories of the real lives of those we teach, of those whose writings fill our days and our nights are out there. And one of them is in your hands.

––––––––––––––

Mark:

I've been reading *The Abandoned Generation* by Willimon and Naylor. There are a bunch of little boxes, asides, throughout the text with remarkable bits inside them. One of them reads:

WHY DID I LEAVE COLLEGE TEACHING?

Why did I leave college teaching? I was teaching a math class for freshmen. One morning I was calling the roll and noted that Jim was absent again.

"Where is Jim?" I asked. The class sat there with a stunned, horrified look on their faces.

"Haven't you heard?" one of them asked.

"Heard what?" I asked.

"Jim died last night. Well, actually, he killed himself, jumped out of his dorm window down to the quad."

I was devastated. Yet more devastation was to come. As Jim's professor, I received absolutely no word from the Dean of Students or anyone else in the administration until three days later when I received a terse note which read, "Jim Smith has withdrawn from the University. Please note whether he withdrew from your course with a Pass or a Fail."

I left teaching the next year.

Martha Ann, describing her experience as a mathematics professor at a large southern public university [italics in the original]. (103)

Mark, Martha Ann's experience may be an extreme example of institutional indifference, but the point here is that there is an awful paradox at work in institutions of higher education. At the same time that the academy "professes" humanity and learning, it too often (once is too often) overlooks the very humans to which it "owes" its existence.

To John Jay's credit, when a popular former student council president committed suicide last year, the administration and faculty joined together not only to notify everyone in a remarkably sensitive manner, we also participated in a moving, collective vigil with students, faculty and administration amply represented.

Here's another quote from Willimon and Naylor, something dear to your own heart:

In no way will tinkering with the curriculum alone change American higher education. Sometimes we have been guilty of refurbishing the curriculum because that was much easier than addressing tough personnel matters in the faculty. A new curriculum, administered by faculty with the same old attitudes, will be little innovation at all. (140)

Michael

Michael:

I have read a terrific essay on teaching and on the meaning of caring for students. It is "Teaching Other People's Children" by Emily Jessup and Marion Lardner, a university professor and a kindergarten teacher.

Moving stories of real people. Lardner tells of Christopher, who falls asleep in kindergarten because his mother has to care for grandchildren as well as him, getting him to sleep later than she would like; Elaine, whose mom is a bag-lady; Ronald, acting out in school, and living in a shelter, with his mother and brothers and sisters, away from an abusive father. Emily Jessup, at the university, writes:

> *The most important part of my teaching is the part that seems hardest to justify. I'm glad I don't get evaluated on the way I conduct my writing conferences with students. Sometimes for the student's sake or for my own, I perform a little bit: I drop a grammatical term, begin a phrase with 'research suggests' but most of the time, I think, the best work I do is the work for which I have not been trained. I listen, I smile, I ask questions,* . . . [her italics] (202)

Michael, finding pieces of writing like this is a joy. They are truths that open up the phenomenologically overloaded act of teaching. They do not set out to present answers to teaching problems or rhetorical analyses of student texts, or ethnographic recording and sorting into categories/codes/interpretations of experience, or cultural studies ending in theories of culture that read like foundational mechanisms which the studies themselves make possible in the first place. Reading an article like this *is* experience. The pained and joyful rendering of moments in teaching. A work. An artful foregrounding of the realities of the classroom.

> We never have enough time or energy to listen to everybody. Inevitably, there will be a story that we do not have time to hear, or we find persons in our classroom with whom we cannot form a relationship, because they are hostile or withdrawn, perhaps because we are simply too tired. Then, when we begin to accept a certain percentage of loss, when we become realistic about what a teacher can do, we have created yet another barrier. Even when we are trying desperately to hold to the idea of reaching each student, we may fail. We may misread our students, come to an overhasty conclusion about what they need from us. And finally, because attentive teaching is so personal, because it is teaching informed with both reason and love, it often feels awkward and is hard to describe. (198)

Oh—and I have forgotten to mention that the chapter is written as a series of letters and journal entries and accompanying interpretive sections.

Is my letter here a hymn of praise? Why not? How is this for an educational theory?: "As teachers, we need to come to know the people whose worlds we share as best we can. We can start by listening and watching. We can ask our students and our children to help us figure out how to become better teachers. We can share what we are learning with each other" (206).

Mark

Mark:

One of the passages you quoted from Jessup and Lardner struck a nerve. They wrote: "when we become realistic about what a teacher can do, we have created yet another barrier" (198). On the one hand, I would respond to this by arguing that we *have to be* realistic about what we can and can't do as teachers. Otherwise, our frustrations mount, and our efforts start to seem inadequate. But, on the other hand, there's a big part of me that shares Jessup and Lardner's view. I think I understand them to mean that if we stop imagining new ways of working with students, if we give up on the idea of working *with* students in our own efforts to "become better teachers," then we are putting obstacles between ourselves and our students and between students and their possibilities for learning.

I know I don't want to stop dreaming up challenging projects, innovative classrooms and courses, and pushing my students to become more and more competent, and confident, in tackling difficult work. At the same time, where do we draw the line between encouraging students to grapple with rewarding-but-difficult projects and subjecting our students to experiences that make their lives more difficult?

Michael

_____

The IUP/JJC Interstate Neighborhood Project

Michael:

I'm preparing my fall graduate course, Rhetorical Traditions, and was writing to Elspeth [Stuckey] about setting up a correspondence between her elementary students and my graduate students [as part of Elspeth's South Carolina Cross-Age Tutoring Project] when it occurred to me that, Michael, we both have students, too! What about it? What sort of vision might our students make with each other? What if a class of yours and a class of mine (maybe undergrad) wrote a book together like mine do every semester?

Mark

_____

Mark:

Sounds good. Let's devise a project with our Research Writing students for which they would research and write about their ideas of community, a better world, even just a better neighborhood. They could write to each other, New York to Pennsylvania, and produce some sort of booklet on communities or neighborhoods. Philip Abbot says, "social space must be won . . . wrested and torn away from economic and political institutions" (169). Do our students (do we, for that matter) have a chance to win social space for themselves and for their children? Abbot also says we have achieved a culture of "intimate anonymity" (165). Is this something to resist?

Michael

Michael:

I'm there! Drafts of and contributions to the book could pass back and forth via overnight mail.[1]

Back to our classes. I think the neighborhood theme can work, though we will have to talk about how. I never assign readings in my research writing classes—or topics for that matter. This is going to mean quite a change for me—which is good—except that I am also uncomfortable about making any required texts the center of my students' attentions for the semester. Hmmm. It can be worked out though.

Getting excited yet? I am. Talk soon.

Mark

One semester, we "joined" Mark's 202 Research Writing class and Michael's 102 Research Writing class. In Mark's section, the students were primarily white, working class, sons and daughters of miners and steel workers, small-town, college residents. In Michael's section, the students were primarily African American, Caribbean, Latina and Latino city residents, who commuted from the five boroughs of New York City.[2] We linked our two classes through mail, electronic mail, and through our own conversations, which we reported to each other's classes. After much discussion, we decided to have our students investigate some of the features, residents, and histories of their neighborhoods, as well as ideas and plans for future ones. Our goals were to provide students with opportunities to conduct primary, as well as secondary, research, and to present their findings in letters and a collectively authored book. In this book, students would collaborate in defining "neighborhood"—formally and creatively. They would write up portraits of neighborhood residents and create brief narratives of their neighborhoods. In their collaborations, they would explore differences among neighborhoods. They would try to identify and investigate critical issues in their neighborhoods and, finally, they would collaborate to design or describe plans for better neighborhoods.

Along the way, students would each keep a research notebook in which they recorded their thinking and reading, as well as their insights about researching.[3]

During the course of the semester, the two groups developed a kind of friendship in which they taught each other about the places and ways in which they live. In many cases, what each learned about the other was surprising, sometimes shocking. In every case, the correspondence between students was the favorite part of the class.

This design was a departure from both of our typical research writing classes. Mark does not usually assign readings, content, or research topics. Instead, his students write and desktop publish two projects: a research report, which may take creative as well as traditional forms, on a subject of each student's choosing, and a magazine project, in which students all work together to write articles and columns, and make layout and other creative decisions to produce a class magazine. Even in this project, the students determine—through whole class investigation and discussion, and with Mark's guidance—the content of the magazine. (The last two of these magazines have been on popular culture and contained researched articles on everything from social issues to lifestyles and interviews with students, professors, and national figures such as Kevin McClatchey, owner of the Pittsburgh Pirates, on his own college career, and Ian McKaye of Fugazi, on music and politics.) In Michael's typical research-writing course, the required second semester of freshman composition, students typically do extensive library research and write several individually authored research papers on literature or on social issues, and, always, students write at least one collaborative paper or project that uses primary and secondary sources. (These projects are discussed in detail in Part 5.) For this shift away from the departmental curriculum, Michael approached his departmental Chair with an outline of the proposed course. The Chair enthusiastically supported the idea.

Now, of course, we had to present this idea on the first day of our classes. As it turned out, our students were even more enthusiastic than we had hoped they would be. They were excited at the prospect of working with students from another state, and they were intrigued by the idea of producing a collaborative book on the subject of neighborhoods.

So, the first thing we had to do was set up writing partnerships so that each of our students would have one or more interstate partners. To do this, we paired our students randomly. Then, through discussions between ourselves and with our students, we decided that everyone would exchange at least two letters, although many opted to continue the correspondence beyond that. In the first letter, they would introduce themselves and outline their impressions of what the project would involve. In the second letter, they would describe in detail their neighborhoods, their impressions and memories of having lived in these places, and, if they wished, include photographs, maps, and other materials they wanted to share. At any point, students could update one another on their progress, not only in learning more and more about their own neighborhoods, but in coming up with ideas for ways to create better ones.

Mark:

Monday. I just met with my first 102 class.

Many asked useful questions about logistics ("how can we do this kind of work in a normal classroom?") and about time ("is there really time to learn everything about making a book?"). They were certainly interested in the idea of thinking about their neighborhoods and their lives.

Michael

Mark:

Wednesday. Met with my class a second time. We began to generate things to observe about neighborhoods and to start thinking about the first batch of letters. For starters, they're going to draw floor plans of their dwellings. My students are also going to describe a typical day in their neighborhood, and they each plan to learn at least one "fact" about the neighborhood that will require them to research it. It might be the population, the number of parks, the tax-base, the relation of the neighborhood to recent current events, and so on.

I've suggested that my students consider the question of how they know where the border(s) are of their neighborhood—would someone else (not from the 'hood) know these limits? How?

Good luck with your 202 research writing class tomorrow. From here, it looks like a fairly typical group—serious urban dwellers.

Michael

Michael:

Thursday. I finally had my first 202 class today. Yours are serious urban dwellers. Mine are seriously rural. They wanted to know about John Jay and the students there. And they made a quick list of things to have you say to your students for them:

> Sounds exciting. Let's get started.
>
> Sounds great.
>
> Wow (meaning this seems important). [We added this explanation of "wow" after discussing whether the term would be sufficiently clear to an audience they didn't know. Their first class lesson in rhetorical awareness!]
>
> This is REALLY going to be a learning experience.
>
> It's scary because we don't know you and how you were taught to write and think.
>
> We don't have your experiences.
>
> Welcome.

Michael, between you and me, I think my students were afraid that they might not be good enough writers, that your students would think they are stupid or somehow inadequate. They don't want to let your students down.

Mark

―――――――――――――

Mark:

Please reassure your students that mine are not already expert writers. In fact, many are second semester freshmen who may or may not have done particularly well in their freshman comp. class. A number are returning (older) students who have not done much writing in years. Your students may be surprised at how many mistakes and, for example, how much Spanish-inflected grammar they see.

Michael

―――――――――――――

Michael:

Today my students spent a fair amount of time fretting about semantics. What do the words "neighborhood" and "community" mean? Or "what is the focus of the project, our neighborhoods or us?"

I suggested a format, for the format minded, for the first letters. (I cribbed it from you, mostly.):

1) Describe where you live.

2) Provide floor plans, maps, photos, etc.

3) Describe a typical day in your neighborhood/location.

4) Learn at least one fact you didn't know.

Some will write about the towns they come from and some about their dorms or apartments at IUP. (I like that they had to consider where they are "from" in this way.) I see no reason to make them all write about home OR school. Also, for some the word "neighborhood" hardly seems to apply to the places they call home when there may not be another house for five or ten miles. Seems like a useful confusion.

Next, we began to talk about typical days in our neighborhoods/locations—so many of the rural students said much the same thing: "At home I get up around noon, watch soaps, eat, and go out at 5 or 6 and meet friends and get drunk until 3 or 4 AM, go home, and start over." A dawning awareness about the nature of their lives seemed to come over the room. What my students will do with this new vision, I don't know. Class was over. I wish we had had another hour to work together. I sensed they did, too. It's as if the students had discovered more knowledge than they could incorporate into their conceptions of themselves in one class period.

Mark

Our students seemed genuinely eager to work on preparing drafts and gathering information. They discussed what they wanted to accomplish in their letters. In small groups and whole class discussions, they talked about visiting historical societies and gathering informational pamphlets. They shared ideas about who they wanted to interview to get inside information about their home towns or neighborhoods. They considered how to find the people who would be the most knowledgeable. They wanted to do everything right. They wanted to let their correspondents in on the reality of their lives. In fact, they ended up *adding to* the realities. Our students took it upon themselves to visit museums, government buildings, tourist spots, landmarks, and districts so they could not only have a better sense of how to describe their environments to their partners, but to more fully develop their own neighborhood identities.

Michael:

I imagine your students are as excited as mine. In fact, you would have loved how they fussed over the photos they took of themselves, their neighborhoods, etc. They even got into groups and signed their pictures. And the stuff they are sending—everything from the letters to photos to tourist brochures to maps to floor plans—terrific energy. They told me they didn't want to switch partners for the next letters. One said he wanted to keep and develop this new friendship.

Yesterday, when my students saw the mailing list, they immediately began practicing the names, some giggling, asking each other questions about them—finally one brave guy, Keith, asked, "Is my partner a boy or a girl?" We all laughed. One of them said, "There sure are a lot of Hispanic names here." I said, "What do you think about that?" He said, "I like it." I asked Melissa who was shaking her head yes, "Melissa, why do you like it?" She said, "Because they are different from us." Michael, this was one of those small moments—an incremental step, I think, toward an understanding of what can be learned from the study of difference. I can't wait to see where this journey will lead.

Mark

Letters of Introduction

Dear Consuela:

Hello, my name is Kelly. I am nineteen years old, and a sophomore here at Indiana University of PA.[4]

When I hear the word neighborhood, I can't help but think of my hometown. Coral has five streets and at least fourteen houses on each side of the street. There are also five alleys that divide the backyards of each house. Coral use to be a coke oven town. Today you can still see the area where there use to be a coke oven, way up on the hill and deep into the woods.

The people of Coral are all really nice. We all know each other and most of the time it is like we are just one big family. When my family and I go away on vacation, our neighbors always watch our house for us.

I have four best friends. Most of the time we would go out around 8:00 pm, and drive around. We would meet other kids and go out on a back road or in the woods, and sit around and talk about anything that comes to our mind as we drink. Most of the time we drink, because there isn't anything else for us to do.

Kelly

Dear Kelly:

Hello! My name is Consuela my ethnic background is Hispanic. My parents are from Honduras but I was born in Brooklyn, New York. I am twenty years old. Once a month I like to go out to clubs to dance all night to get the tension out of my system. Monday through Thursday I go to school. On a typical Monday morning I feel exhausted and angry. Monday mornings is a hassle in New York City. Everyone is in a rush because they are running late. Every Monday morning I have to run to catch the train. Once I am on the train I have to fight my way in to get a spot. On a typical Sunday morning I go to church.

I live in Brooklyn, in Bed–Stuy short for Bedford–Stuyvesant. People who live in this community are African Americans and Puerto Ricans. Bed–Stuy is huge. There are like around ten housing projects in Bed–Stuy. The housing projects in which I live is called Sumner Projects.

I do not hang-out in my projects. From school or from wherever I am coming from I go straight home and I do not come out until the next day. The drug-dealers consider themselves the owners of Bed-Stuy. They sell drugs and guns to children. There are two parks in Sumner Projects. The sad thing is that you do not see children playing in the parks. Instead you would see young people every day destroying their lives by sniffing cocaine, smoking marijuana, or smoking crack. Those teenagers have taken the parks away from our children. It breaks my heart seeing young people destroying their lives with that garbage.

Just two weeks ago on my way to school a young girl like around sixteen tried to sell her baby to me for thirty dollars for she could get some money to buy some cocaine. The next day I heard, she sold her baby for twenty dollars and died from a drug overdose. Yesterday right across a street from my building an eight year old shot his best friend in the chest just because he was upset with him. The eight year old got the gun from a hustler who rent it to him for ten dollars. Now a little boy is fighting for his life in a hospital bed. These hustlers are on every corner of the street bribing children to buy drugs, sell drugs, or to buy guns. Are there drug dealers selling drugs or guns to the children of your neighborhoods? What ethnic background do the people in your neighborhood come from?

It is not easy living in the projects. Every day we have to struggle to survive. We face death every single day. Every day we are losing children that do not even reach the age of twenty-one. Life is not easy, and life is not a guarantee with just one bullet threw your chest your life is over.

Consuela

In Mark's class the students were silently reading, riveted to the letters in their hands, which they read over and over again. Mark noticed that Kelly looked particularly troubled. She spoke to no one. After a while, she looked up and said, "I can't believe this."

Mark asked if she wanted to read her letter or some part of it to the class.

She said, "You better read it first."

Mark did, and then she did, aloud.

The class was silent.

In Michael's room, after his class had likewise privately read, shared their letters with their friends, and then moved toward discussion, Consuela was listening to her classmates talking about the fact that so many of the IUP letters spoke of drinking. She read Kelly's description about kids getting drunk in the woods. Some of her classmates shook their heads.

Dear Consuela:

My ethnic background is Slovak, but I was born in this area. My grandparents came over on a boat from Czechoslovakia, with high expectations of the American Dream, and I had to hear this story at least a million times when I was growing up.

I was surprised to hear how much violence there is in your neighborhood. As I said in my previous letter, my neighborhood is really small, and all that are in it is some houses and a church. Everyone knows everyone in my neighborhood and everybody goes about their own business. This is why I think there isn't any violence. I can't image not going into your parks. In the summer, I would go for walks around my neighborhood, and most of the time, my family and I don't lock our doors at night.

There isn't any problems with drugs or guns in our neighborhood, or if there is I don't know about it. The most serious problem in the area is alcohol. It seems that all you ever hear anymore is about drinking, or driving and drinking. Today, kids seem to start drinking at an earlier age, and most of the time, it is teenagers that are getting caught for driving drunk. I don't get drunk and I hate being around people that are drunk. A member of my family is an alcoholic, and I see how he acts and that is the last person I want to be like.

Kelly

Dear Kelly:

I hope I did not scare you in the first letter that you received from me.

I have been living in Bed–Stuy for twenty years now and consider Bed-Stuy as being a neighborhood that has problems. The three major problems that are in Bed-Stuy are teenage pregnancy, drugs, and crime.

In Bed-Stuy the community leaders are building five community centers for the young people. These centers are for the youngsters of Bed-Stuy so they

could stay off the streets and stay out of trouble. Hopefully once the centers are built there would be less crime and drug problems in Bed-Stuy. On Sunday I went to a youth meeting in the community center that we have in Sumner. In the youth meeting there are young people from ages (12–25) who get together to find solutions on ways how they can live in a better community. The burglaries in apartments have gone down because we organized a Neighborhood Crime Watch Program, so that has helped a lot of people living in the community. We are trying to unite all the African Americans and the Hispanics in one. So that we as a family can take violence and drug-dealers out of our neighborhood. We are sick of hearing the same thing over and over again. It is time we get our neighborhood back.
—What is a coke oven?
—How many people are living in Coral?

Consuela

Dear Consuela:

A coke oven is an oven that used to burn coal in it, to make coke. Then the coke was used in the steel mills. As I said before, Coral is a small town. It only has a population approximate of 325 people.

Some of the problems in your neighborhood are completely different from the ones in my neighborhood. Most of the problems are as I said before, alcohol, and unemployment. I think the reason why alcohol is such a big problem is because a lot of people are not happy with their lives. The unemployment rate is so high in this area, a lot of the [local population] don't have a job and they don't know how they are going to be able to support their families, so they turn to alcohol all of the time just to forget about their problems.

Kelly

Michael:

I asked my students to describe their conceptions of your students. Here is their brainstormed, collective list:

Cool
Interesting
Varied backgrounds
Hard-ass
People we envy
Loud
Streetwise
From fast paced environment
Living real lives

This came about just before a class discussion about the lives my students lead. My students are writing about how their lives are so boring and empty that they have little else to do but get drunk.

One student said she hasn't told the half of it. She said she didn't want your students to see the whole truth about her. That led to a discussion about how open my students are prepared to be—basically, they want to know how open your students are going to be—they don't want to go out on the honesty limb alone, I guess. Or as one of them put it, "Will Michael's students tell the truth?"

I warned mine about telling more than they want people to know, but I agreed with the majority of them that we need to be open and honest if we are going to learn much from this project. One of them said, "What's the good of this project if we don't tell the truth?"

Mark

Mark:

I shared your students' descriptions of my students with them and one student, Richard, said, "It's true! We ARE loud; we have to be—this is a noisy city!"

On the other hand, Angela showed me what she had written to Raymond, in your class:

> We received the terms that your class described us as before we received each other's letters. Most of the terms that your class de-scribed us as are true. New Yorkers are loud, streetwise, from fast-paced environments, and we do come from varied backgrounds.
>
> I guess we are loud because we feel we have to survive in a city where everyone practically despises each other. We are streetwise because we hang out in the streets, and observe what's going on in our environment. What makes us different is that we come from various backgrounds, and that's what makes us interesting.
>
> There were other terms such as cool and people we envy. I believe everyone is cool in their own way, you don't have to come from a big-city. Big-city people shouldn't be envied. We live normal lives that become boring after a while.

Mark, I imagine that it comes as quite a surprise to my students that they would be envied for their lives. At the same time, what are they discovering or rediscovering? that their lives are, as your students write about their own, finally boring? So they have discovered that no one is to be envied, or has a fulfilling life? I don't want to believe that this is the only possible discovery to make, yet sometimes I can hardly argue with them.

Michael

Dear Angela:

Hello my name is Ray and I am a 18 year old sophomore at I.U.P.

A typical day for me in my personal hell also known as my neighborhood starts around noon when I get up. Than I watch soap operas until about 2:00 p.m. than I hang out or play basketball or something until about 6:00 p.m. Than I eat dinner and go out for the night where I probably go ride around and than hang out at someone's house and drink some beer until I stumble in at 2:00 a.m. and start over again the next day.

I couldn't really think of anything historical that happened in the oppressive neighborhood of Crafton probably because it is so small. However I do remember something that happened when I was younger that really changed our neighborhood. A small girl I can't really recall her name was reported missing and for a couple of years the police could'nt find her. Than one day the police found the remains of her body buried in my next door neighbors back yard. After that things were never the same. No one really trusted anyone and I remember we were'nt allowed to play over any of our friends houses after that.

Here at school I live in an off campus apartment which I call home because I spend more time here than I do at home. I share my apartment with three other guys. We all get along pretty well. Our place just looks like a bachelor pad. There are beer bottles all over the place even in the aquarium. Our refridgerator does'nt have anything in it except more beer, some cheese and a fuzzy bowl that I think used to be spaghetti. Even as I write there is a pile of dirty dishes stagnating in the sink. Our place isn't really that bad usually because we can always find someone to clean it for us.

I don't know if this is what our letter is supposed to sound like but it's the best that I can do. After all I'm not an english major or anything to tell you the truth this is the first letter that I have ever written.

Raymond

Dear Raymond:

My name is Angela, I am 19 years old, and I am at my second year at John Jay College. My major is Criminal Justice. My goals are to accomplish four years, receive my Bachelors, then continue on to my Masters. Hopefully go on to law school and work for a major law corporation.

Reading over your letter, you gave me the impression that not only you didn't want to write to me, but that you have a negative way of looking at things. You sort of tried to impress me by your lifestyle of just drinking and hanging out. I'm sorry if I'm blunt but that's my nature. I'm sure there's more to your life than watching soaps and drinking beers, and I think you should share it. Anyway it was nice to receive a letter from you.

Angela

Dear Angela:

Hello how are you doing, fine I hope. I would like to start my second letter
by apologizing for my first. I did not mean to offend you. However now that I
have completely alienated you I suppose that I have your attention. Please
bear with me as I try not to stick my foot in my mouth again, which is hard for
me to do because it comes so naturally to me.

What impressed me so much was how serious you are about the project
that it made me realize that I better get my act together in order not to short
change either of us. It's kind of ironic that we were picked to be partners
because we appear to be complete opposites. Not that it's bad or anything it's
just that we are two completely different people. You seem to be more serious
about everything then I am. I started out to be really serious about school,
then I started to party more. Before long the nights started to get longer and
longer and the days shorter and shorter, and before I knew it my life turned
into one long night followed by a few comatose daylight hours. My whole
purpose in life seems to be to have as much as fun as I can as long as I can
then just fade away. From reading your letter it seems that you have your
whole life planned out, while my life on the other hand lacks anything that
even remotely resembles direction.

I grew up in projects much like the ones in New York I'm sure, over-
crowded, rundown, and dangerous are the words that come to mind when I
think of this place. Money was tight even more then usual because what
money there was had to provide for my two brothers two sisters, and myself.
However, even though my mother had a tough time supporting all of us by
herself she never denied me anything while growing up and sometimes I felt a
sort of dislike displayed towards me from my siblings and that really hurt me
bad.

Growing up in a neighborhood where I probably saw some form of violence
every single day I was forced to grow up alot faster that most kids who lived in
little white houses with white picket fences. I was a latch-key kid for as long as
I remember and that goes back to at least third grade (but when you can't
afford a baby sitter what can you do).

By the age of twelve the old neighborhood had gotten too dangerous to
raise a boy my age in, because gangs had started to show their first signs we
packed up and moved to my present neighborhood.

Since I had no time to play I was labeled as different and got no respect
from other kids until I started to hit anyone who said anything to me in the
mouth. After that they straightened up real quick and started to realize that I
was not to be f____ed with.

As far as things go around my Present neighborhood that I didn't say last
time. There are two different kinds of houses old three story brick houses like
mine and newer one story aluminum siding houses that were just built about
seven years ago. The newer ones were built in only about two days so I'm
waiting for them all to fall apart it ought to be good for a laugh or two.

Raymond

_____

Letters on Neighborhoods

Dear Janine:

I come from a small mining town, called Bakerton, with a population of 835 people. When the town first started, a mining company called Barnes and Tucker was established to create jobs and to remove the coal deposits that were under the town. After all of the coal was extracted from the ground, the mining company moved on and left a lot of jobless people and mountains of unburnable coal that still remain today. These mountains of coal are bigger than any building in my town and in the summer they give off a rotten odor. The odor comes from the sulfur in the coal. The older people who were able to retire did so, and the rest of the jobless people went to other towns to find jobs such as working in the steel mills or other coal mines. Most people took any job that was available. As for the piles of coal, they are one of the first things I see in the morning from my bedroom window. The little stream that flows through the middle of the town has turned orange from the sulfur in the coal. I feel as if the mining company ripped the town off; they came and got what they wanted and left the town a mess. I can't stand to see the piles of coal outside my window.

I am here because I want to show my parents that I am capable of graduating from college, something they have never done. My mom has worked in a dress factory all of her life and will be there until she can retire. My real father graduated from high school and went to work in the mines until he got hurt. He got hurt so badly he could never return to work. He has been unemployed since he got smashed between the wall and a cart full of coal. Last, but not least, my step-father is a school teacher who has not yet landed a permanent job. He has been getting substitute jobs for the past eight years. Hopefully, he will soon find a permanent position. I would like to tell you some about my family background. When I was nine my mom and dad got a divorce. I am happy now, but back then I was very sad. I can now see that the divorce was the best thing my parents could have done, because all they did was verbally and physically fight with one another. This was hard on my brother and I but we managed to trudge through it all. When my parents would start fighting, I would hide my brother under the bed and I would stand between my mom and dad in order to get them to stop fighting. This usually worked but there were a few times where I just got pushed out of the way, but I would get up and be standing between them before either of them could hit the other again. Events like this happened every two or three times a week for almost two years. There were very few happy times in my family and the ones we had, I can't remember because there were so many traumatic times.

Josh

Dear Josh:

I live on Jamaica Avenue in Woodhaven, which is a little area of Queens. There are many negatives in living in the city but I have to say I would not want to live anywhere else. We have our share of problems but it does not stop people from doing their jobs. One problem is crime; You really have to be careful when you are out. Stores are held up once in a while, people on streets get mugged, this is a sad story, but people have to go on with their lives. The other problem is Drugs: It's a real shame when you walk down the street and there are drug pushers on the street. You know they are there but you really can't say anything because you would probably end up dead. I really don't think about it much because I don't want to get myself down. The way I see it is that I am not going to let this get me down, I am going to get myself out of this neighborhood and have a better life.

Janine

Dear Nina:

My name is James, and I am 20 years old. I hail from a small town in Western Pennsylvania.

Almost the entire population is made up of hard working, middle-class families, who depend entirely on the steel mill to earn a living. You see, a major steel company based in my town specialized in stainless steel and specialty steels. Everyone in my town is, in some way, connected to the mill, and I can say, without hesitation, that if the steel mill were ever to go under or relocate, my town would become a forgotten ghost town.

I grew up on the outskirts of town, if you can even call it that. There are miles and miles of trees, fields and creeks, excellent for hunting, hiking, fishing, or just a stroll in the woods. The average distance between houses is about 200 yards.

After dinner I would lie around for a while and then get showered and ready to go out at around 9 PM. We would take a ride around town, just cruising to see if other old high school friends were out, and then proceed to either go to a bar in town or get some beer and head down the "The River". The River as we know it has been a local gathering place for years and years. Since the beginning of time, teenagers have made the journey down to the train tracks beside the river, which are not used anymore, to partake in a night long drinking frenzy. The police would never bother us there. It was a place for camaraderie and good times. I would usually get home around 2:00 in the morning, go to bed and get up four hours later to do the same thing over and over again. That's pretty much what life is like here, a small, humble town I call home.

James

Dear James:

    In reading the description of your neighborhood, it is all new to me. Since I am from such a diverse area it is very hard to imagine how a whole town relies on one company for work. Where I live my neighbors all have different types of jobs in different companies and agencies. I am under the impression that life in [your town] is sweet and simplistic.

    We have similar lifestyles; for one, we both go to college. The parties I attend are like the one in the video [you sent us of your fraternity house and your parties]. We drink beer from a funnel, also that is the quickest way to get wasted. My friends and I like to drink Tequila, and after a few shots we all start telling everyone how much we love them and every single problem we've had since childhood.

    In class, Professor Blitz read the description that your class had of mine. This is what I wrote in my notebook about the students in Pennsylvania: "My personal view about the students that we are writing to is that they are a lot like us. For one they are in college seeking an education to better their lives or social status. Style is what you make of it, different people have different styles. Everyone likes to party regardless of where your from. Just everyone has their own definition of what a good party is."

Nina

Mark:

Today, in 102, I played portions of James's video tape. There was a ton of footage of, well, his feet, of sidewalks, of the lawns, of the streets (I mean the actual pavement). We met a few friends, saw gallons of beer, a parade, the inside of James's apartment (some amazement that his roommate is a woman) and general consensus that IUP may be on the moon.

"Shit, don't they believe in black people there?"
"Everybody sounds so drunk all the time!"
"That was cool that he made this tape."
"Do people do anything besides drink beer and say 'Hey, how's it goin?'"
"They have separate buildings for different subjects?!!"
"Everybody's white!"
"Hey! Not one roller-blader?"

We all got a kick out of hearing Steve's letter to Phil, where he wrote:

> Besides the farms, there isn't much of anything in [this town]. We have a bar and the church. So if you don't want to get drunk or pray you are out of luck.
>   Whenever boredom swept over us we resorted to throwing parties. We rolled the kegs into the woods and partied hard with our friends around a huge campfire. We never got busted by the cops because no one heard us or could find us. This is another reason why I love nature.

s next bit, however, was quite sobering:

There are downsides to living anywhere, and [here] is no exception. One problem is the depressed economy. When the mines closed in the early and mid 1900s, money seemed to leave the area. Jobs are hard to come by. I have to work two jobs during the summer so that I can come to school. I am very fortunate [to have two jobs] because a relatively high percentage of the surrounding area is unemployed or on welfare.

Michael

———————————

Dear Mike:

Hello, my name is Christi. I'm 19 years old.

The area in which I live is called Spanish Harlem. In the Spanish language, Spanish Harlem is called "El Barrio" and considered to be from 103d street and 1st avenue all the way to 120th street and Lexington.

The crime and drugs that is around my area doesn't bother me. Well actually it does bother me in the sense that I don't like the fact that it happens, but regardless of whether or not I like it, it will happen anyway. It doesn't bother me in the sense that I do what I have to and I go wherever I need to go and I don't get involved with the drugs or crime.

On 1st Avenue you will find the drug dealers that are on the corner from the morning all the way until the night. First Avenue is like 24hr. drug store where there's always someone on the corner if you need to buy. I live on Second Avenue. Second and Third Avenues are the most decent avenues in Spanish Harlem. The reason why I say this is because there are hardly any drug dealers around, it's quiet, and you don't hear many gun shots or the police sirens as much as you would hear on First Avenue or on Lexington Avenue.

On the corner of the train station I have to pass the drug dealers to go down the stairs leading to the train.

You hardly see the girls around the block because they are usually upstairs taking care of their baby. The only time you would see the girls outside is when they walk by strolling their baby carriages or when they are looking for their boyfriends. The guys are always around the block playing basketball or just hanging out.

Christi

———————————

Dear Jane:

I live in East New York [in Brooklyn]. That's almost next to the beginning of Queens. Usually when my friends hear about THE EAST they ask me if I run when I get out of the [subway] station. They also ask me if there is a lot of beef over where I live at. Sometimes I laugh when I hear things like that. If you were to come visit, I would show you the spots. I would also show you where the kids in my neighborhood be gamin'. When I mean stuff like gamin' and spots' it's terminologies for selling drugs and for just hanging out.

Usually when I don't have anything to do I just go down to my spot on NEW LOTS and ELTON AVENUE. There some stuff that goes down there. If your walking down the block you'll notice a couple of brothers rollin dice they call it "CELO". (It's funny, because I notice that if you're not playing you can't sit around and watch because they don't trust nobody. I mean they could just be rollin and all of a sudden some herb could come and take the ends.

That's why it's not smart to be staring at stuff in this way for a long time. You'll end up playing the victim. Most important, if you do not know where you are going and you are lost, please try not to act like it because especially my way they will see it and play you for the victim.

One thing that I found out about my neighborhood. 30 years ago residence was taken up by the Jewish and Italian[s]. But as the years progressed more and more black and latinos started to take up residence. I looked at a map of East New York and saw a borderline between Brooklyn and Queens. The next day I went to check it out and noticed how the buildings in my area were sort of runned down abandoned.

I noticed how the neighborhoods were dirty and kind of scary looking. But when I passed the border of bklyn and going into Queens their neighborhoods look real nice. It's almost like the minorities can't go any further than Crescent avenue. It's almost like an invisible wall. The Italians on one side and the blacks on the other. Really, Queens is not all white but it's like a safe haven for the upper class. I don't mind it's just that you can really notice the difference in areas.

P.S. Here are a couple of translations for the words I used.
    Gamin: Selling Drugs
    Spots: Hanging out
    Herb: A fool; wimp
    Beef: Trouble
    Ends: Money

Richard

Dear Richard:

I think it's wild that you live in Brooklyn. My best friend attended Pratt University but she only lasted three days because she got mugged and beat around, so she moved back to the great farmlands of [this town].

Jane

Dear Karen:

I am Julio and I am twentyone years old and im currently living with my father in Queens.

While in East New York I lived in a four story building where rent was about four hundred for a two bedroom apartment. It was not the best building but compared to the other buildings that were either burned down or in unlivable conditions, it was great. Just one block away from my house the seventy fifth precinct and one block down on belmont and essex you would have about seven drug dealers selling you crack or anything else for as little as five dollars to as much as one hundred dollars. For fun in brooklyn hanging out side at a corner, playing hand ball or you could go to high land park were how most of the days were spent.

Julio

_____

Dear Julio:

New Sewickley and Unionville, PA, combined are mostly all country with a few convenience stores, gas stations, one elementary school, and the rest well, just homes, farms, cows, trees, and some more cows. It's so quiet that you can hear all the insects and animals making noise around you. So, if you can picture this, this is where I grew up. Not too exciting! The people here are pretty much sedated since not too much happens unless something enlivens them like a rumor about someone which for some reason happens at least a few times a year, but ends up never to be true. Like for instance, a rumor was flying around that this girl had AIDS which was totally wrong, that just got out of hand and people started to talk. Another popular one was that a girl I graduated with was pregnant, as awful as this sounds the rumor was right.

When asked what my typical day is, I have to laugh. I don't have to think twice about my day because most of the time it is so repitious that it does get very boring. Compared to a person that lives in New York City, such as yourself, I'm sure a day in my life will really shock you. Since I have told you about my hometown, I have decided to explain a typical summer day. Well, this summer everyday, I would get out of bed around 6:30, get ready and arrive at the Bank around 8:00. There I was a bank-teller were I would float from bank to bank wherever they needed me. After work about 4:30, I would head on home and relax by reading the newspaper and watch a little television. Once all my friends got home from work, the phones would start ringing and we would start making our plans for the night. Even though there's not really much a person can do around our town, we always seemed to find a party or somewhere to hang out. Depending on the amount of people that would show up at the parties usually determined the amount of beer and alcohol that was there. Only on the weekends are most of the bigger parties. By the end of the week I'm very tired, but I do catch up on my sleep on Sundays. And that is a day in my life, not too amusing right?

Karen

_____

Karen:

I received your letter on Monday and you had a lot to say witch I liked. Now that I read your first letter I feel embarrassed about my letter because you wrote so much and described it so good it made my first letter sound like you were the one living in new York and me living in little old New Sewickly. In my first letter I sounded very dull which I am not but after all I am no writer. in this letter im going to try to give you more details about myself and New York City.

N.Y.C is known mostly for its tall buildings, cites, and its huge amount of diverse people panhandlers, muggers, rapists, etc. but most of all its toughness. One difference about NY and Pa. would be that we don't have cows roaming the city. New York city has a very different life style than over there but I still don't know why you choose to call this "the real life" and why you choose to think the people here are open because we are not.

Julio

_____

Dear John:

I couldn't believe that you and the people in your neighborhood [in Pennsylvania] just started to lock your doors at night and install security systems. I myself have been locking my doors all of my life and security systems are pretty common around here.

Another thing that shocked me was the fact that there are only 25 houses and 55 people in [your town]. On my block alone there are about 50 houses with usually an average of 4 or more people living in each house.

Anna

_____

Dear Anna:

Well, if it shocked you to hear that we are just starting to lock our doors, this will really shock you. In my little part of the world, to date we have not had one burglary, car theft, or actually anything of the sort.

I kind of like the community I live in.

John

_____

Dear Valerie:

I used to live in the projects. What I mean is a group of huge buildings. A building may have 16 to 20 floors and each floor has about 8 apartments. I lived in the projects for 18 years. Because the projects are so big, it gets really crowded sometimes. The elevators would break down a lot, which forced many elderly and handicapped people to walk up the stairs. Another thing that was a problem is that most the kids, teenagers, and sometimes even the adults didn't care, or respect the place they lived or the people that lived there. There was graffiti on the walls, staircases, elevators, and outside the building. There were many cases of vandalism, such as blowing up mailboxes with m-80s, popping the lights in the elevators and the staircases. Many guys sold drugs in and outside of the building. Crackheads (drug users) did drugs, slept, and urinated and took dumps in the stairs, elevators, and on the roof. My parents were really scared for me and my sister. We were all worried for my sister's baby. But all of us were really worried about my mom. See my mom was like the only white person in my building, and more than once many of the dealers expressed their hate for her kind, as they put it. We knew that we had to get out of there, but what really did it for us was when my mom was almost threatened with a gun. One evening when my mom was coming from the parking lot a guy followed her to the building. My mom said she couldn't see him but she heard him cock a gun. That was when we knew we had to get out, so we did. My sister heard about the houses from the church. We signed up for a house, and here I am.

Jessica

Letters on the Neighborhood Book Project

Michael:

Tuesday night, very late. Today, a troubling class experience. A vocal minority in my class expressed their disappointment with the letters they received: they weren't long enough, they didn't get one, the grammar was bad, they weren't personal enough, didn't respond to our letters enough.

A few other students got mad—Valerie said she couldn't understand why people were "nit-picking" about unimportant issues like grammar—why weren't we talking about content? Another student, Sandy, said that some of us were failing to respect our partners and that every one of us could take something of importance from the letter we received.

And Keith read a passage from his partner about the changes in neighborhoods one sees as one travels between the Brooklyn Bridge and the projects. Afterwards a few other students came up to me with terrific passages from their letters or to express their anger at their colleagues.

My students obviously want to know more about your students—their lives and experiences. Also they can't estimate the rhetorical complexity of the demands we are making—to write letters that also fulfill the requirements of academic assignments. They wonder why the letters they are getting are not what they expect and want—yet, they too felt the pressure of trying to write personal letters that also contained research.

Mark

Mark:

In their very sincere and earnest efforts to bridge the distance between IUP and JJC, your students may be expecting that mine will make the identical gestures. They may be discovering that my students seem more guarded than they expected pen-pals to be. Actually, from what I know about my students, your students are getting incredibly candid letters. When I read through the portfolios, I was moved by how forthright so many of these folks have been.[5]

You know, now that I think about it, your students may be just as guarded, just as self-insulating as mine. Your students have written so frequently of boredom and of drinking that it may be too easy to assume that they are being completely up front about the rest of their lives, as well. In fact, I'd now guess that your students are not telling all—the real reasons for all the drinking, the real effects of a home-life that feels so foreign to them once they've spent even a single semester away at the university.

I should also add, with some irony, that my students read through their IUP letters and found a number of the same "problems"!! There were remarks about the grammar, about the repetitions, about the lack of "progress" on the project [the book project of the second half of the semester].

Michael

One of the more objective descriptions of the project's day-to-day "business" was written by a graduate student of Mark's who e-mailed her observations of one particular day in Mark's class to Michael:

> The students were focused on the newly arrived packet of letters from New York and tore into them like little kids opening Christmas presents. Those who did not receive a letter were truly upset and disappointed—though I think they really did try to understand that sometimes "things happen." Only a couple students sounded a bit unforgiving: "If WE can get all OUR letters sent out, why can't THEY? WE have problems too; [student's name] was even sick, and HE got HIS done!" The students who received extra goodies in their letters (maps, pictures, etc.) were really proud and showed off the items to the rest of the class.

After reading her letter, one female student whined: "I sent him 12 pages; look what he said about my accident—one sentence, 'I'm glad you're alive.' Then he talks about sports!" One soft-spoken young woman commented: "I'm from New England. We're really reserved up there—not like here. We should focus on that which is helpful."

Soon the Little Grammarian came out of a few students: "He spells the word which with a 't'!" A couple students agreed that punctuation, spelling, and grammar were problematic; they felt their letters were mechanically superior to those they had received. Finally, one woman made an announcement: "Some of you are not going to like what I have to say." (Mark called a brief time-out to make certain no one was going to hold a grudge, though I think the student was going to say what she had to say come hell or high water.) "Some of you are being too nit-picky. What matters most is MEANING. If you can understand the letter, that's what's most important."

One woman confidently summed things up by pointing out that Indiana and New York were totally different and that the two groups were looking at everything from entirely different perspectives, and everyone should just realize this fact and accept it. A young man added that several students were expecting SO MUCH from their correspondents and that it was not really fair to be upset if some correspondents didn't live up to their expectations.

The students loved the photos. Each one anxiously looked for the face of her correspondent.

A few brought up good questions: How do different neighborhoods happen? Why does a drug pusher stand on this corner but not on the one across the street? Why are the police quick to respond in this neighborhood but not in that one? Is there such a thing as a neighbor-hood attitude? Is the difference between neighborhoods an indication of class? wealth? race? Students thought it was reasonable to create a book with two sections, a New York section and an Indiana section. There seemed to be a universal consensus on this proposal.

Mark:

My students would be surprised to know that your students do not see the nearly total effort mine are making to be forthcoming. There are a couple of miracles happening that I want to alert you to: Ernesto may say fewer than 100 words per day. And yet he is doing his damnedest to come across to his IUP partners. Miguel has done reasonably well in keeping his enormous (if good natured) ego in check because he wants to respect his partner. Julio was, so far as I can tell, allowed to graduate high school without being able to write a complete sentence or to read aloud. Angela—who I consider to be one of the most active participants—has, according to her, never until this semester taken her education seriously—she's always been intensely cynical about it. Anthony is so quiet, so self-effacing, and so accustomed to total anonymity, I'm in awe of his struggle to break his own insularity. Richard is amazed at the immaturity of the student with whom he is corresponding, and yet he speaks glowingly of that student's willingness to try to understand him (Richard) from such a different time of life. Geneva is in the thicket of a violent domestic life which has her on the run—still, she has not wanted to "abandon" her IUP partnership. Christi has had a run of rotten health, but she, too, is exhausting herself to keep things going.

There is more; there is always more. Maybe you can convey to your students—as I convey to mine about yours—that there is no way to know, even from the letters themselves, what factors must converge for one human being to make an effort to cover the distance, to connect to another person.

Michael

Dear Tom:

My building overlooks the Henry Hudson River. I have been living in this building for nineteen years. I have watch my building changed. The people that lived in my neighborhood were Irish. Now there are Spanish, black, a few white and Chinese families. There are a lot of working people in my building. My building used to have a doorman. Now we have security guards.

In my personal opinion, I feel this project is going well. It is very different from my other courses. Two classes in different environments discussing neighborhoods, family, and all the things we go through living in a community and trying to make it better. It's great! I want to see some pictures of your neighborhood. Your family and friends. I will still be gathering information for the next letter. I want to find out why my building is called the Promenade. How did it come about? I hope I will gather a lot more information about my neighborhood for the class and for myself.

Wanda

Dear Angela:

The neighborhood here [Indiana, PA] is different from my neighborhood at home [Philadelphia, PA]. For instance, at night it gets very quiet and very dark since it seems that in Indiana, the people here don't care too much about street lights. At night if I have to walk alone, you better believe that I get from point A to point B in a matter of minutes. An example of this is the Oak Grove at I.U.P. The Oak Grove is the main walkway on campus that allows students to go from place to another. It's a park with many trees, walking paths, and a few benches. It has lighting, but if you are walking alone late at night, it can be a frightening experience. Most of the people here aren't afraid of walking around at night or leaving their doors unlocked. I tell them that no matter where I am, it's better to be safe than sorry. For instance, my roommates have a habit of leaving the door unlocked so that any Tom, Dick, or Harry can walk in. I know I act this way because living in a neighborhood like mine in Philadelphia teaches you that everyone cannot be trusted.

Rita

Letters of Evaluation

As we would find throughout the project, our students managed to fill their letters with information on a surprising number of levels. Already we had seen writing about physical features of the neighborhoods as well as accounts of some of the people with whom our students live. Sometimes students would simply describe their daily routines, providing vivid portraits of what they regarded as business as usual. For example, one of Michael's students wrote:

> I am a 20 year old mother of two. I have two boys, the eldest is four years old, and the other is a four month old infant.
> During one of my typical days I travel from the Bronx to Manhattan by train. Going from the Bronx to Manhattan is totally different because the Bronx has more small buildings and very few projects, more streets, and less motivation. You see lots of stores on each corner. As I take the train to my mother's, I take three underground trains, then I get off, enter my mother's house to drop off my baby, and take the eldest to school. Then I go off to the bus which I take [to] the cross-town bus to the west side, I transfer to another bus until it leaves me right in front of [John Jay College]. I have school from Monday-Thursday afternoons, and I work from Monday-Thursday mornings. I have Fridays off, but I still have to get up to take my son to school by 8:40 am, then I rest until 2:45 pm. Sometimes I don't rest because I have appointments I schedule for Fridays because I don't like to miss out of work or school. And this would be a typical day for me.

In the exchange between Kelly and Consuela, we also found a remarkable openness in trying to interpret the social realities of neighborhood experiences. Kelly may not have studied a great deal of social science, yet she had real insights into the relationship between unemployment, boredom, drinking, and apathy. Consuela wrote about community action and the need for young people to play a more active role in reshaping their neighborhoods. It is hard for us to imagine a better way for our students to learn about social issues, community, the nature of everyday urban and rural life, as well as the researching of each, than through this kind of caring and respectful interchange.

Students didn't always know how to respond to one another. They certainly wanted to, but occasionally, we found, letters seemed to "miss" one another somewhat. While some students engaged in an interconnected dialogue, others mostly exchanged somewhat random bits of information about school, home, schedules, families. We did not see this as a weakness in the process; rather, we pointed out to those students who received letters that sometimes seemed unrelated to ones they'd sent that doing research often entails accumulating odd pieces of information and insight toward a larger picture or toward a later interpretation.

Michael:

Today I asked my EN 202 students to create a set of criteria by which they wanted their letter portfolios to be graded. I will collect them next week. Here's a list of these criteria:

Completeness: the letters don't have holes—information that should have been included—or info suggested but not included

Creativity/Personality

Descriptiveness/Effort

Grammar and Punctuation—with the realization that these are personal letters

Length

Clarity—they make sense as personal letters

Politeness/Respect for the Other Letter Writer

Research

What do you think?

Mark

Mark:

It occurred to me, today, that I don't know how to evaluate the portfolios of letters my students are assembling and handing in next time. I know there are criteria to be upheld, but somehow it almost seems unfair to grade these earnest endeavors to make contact with the aliens. As I look through the batch of letters, I'm touched by the sincerity and, in most cases, newfound creativity my students are showing. I hate to discourage any of it. But we promised them grades, and they want grades and they need grades.

I've ended up establishing the five criteria as follows:

> Overall organization within the two letters
>
> Evidence of planning, revision, editing, reconsidering for final drafts
>
> Effectiveness of the follow up (second) letter as pertaining to the first partner-letter
>
> Evidence of appropriate reading/research in second letter
>
> Language skills (diction, grammar, punctuation, structure, etc.)*

*the last item was at the "insistence" of students—actually, they reached consensus only on that item of the student-generated criteria—can you believe it? They really are trained in the minutiae, aren't they?

And so, each criterion received 0, 1, 2, 3, 4 points—the total (max.) of 20 to equal the 20% of the final grade, as promised in the syllabus.

I've given scores ranging from 8 to 20. Most seem to be falling in the 14–18 zone. This grading seems wrong and hypocritical. Why? I'm really not sure, but I think it's because I know how much labor was involved—far more than I even expected (I expected a lot). I also wish my students did not have to reduce their hard work and their discoveries to a numerical reward (or punishment) system. True, I'll be talking to each of them individually about all their work, but this is another time when scholastic evaluation seems so disappointing and inadequate.

Michael

Michael:

My grading of my students' letter portfolios is done. I used the criteria my students named plus one of my own—ten criteria—and I don't feel good about the grades. I agree with you. It feels all wrong—and yet I guess I feel I did as well as I could. I think we should have thought the problem of grading through more thoroughly. If only teaching this class were the only thing we had to do this semester! Still there are, finally, no excuses that absolve. I wish we had seen in advance the tension we feel right now and had, I don't know, graded more holistically somehow. (Perhaps no matter what we had done, it would not seem right to apply a grading apparatus or assign a grade to this sort of humanistic work.) Maybe a simple contract: you get an A if you complete the work. I don't know.

Mark

Mark:

I've been reading through my students' notebooks that they kept throughout the semester. I want to excerpt some things for you:

> Where I live, about Mt. Sinai Hospital, the Jews are greedy, want money, they're prejudism there against minorities, especially with medicaid, the insurance because of private rooms, different floors, better treatment.

> One thing I know that's a big problem around my neighborhood is the lack of security. Our [housing] projects has no kind of security for us tenants who pay rent and who have to come in and out of our buildings every day. We need security from all of the violence that these drug dealers around our neighborhood bring. From all of the robbers and rapists . . . It has affected me. I'm a victim of rape. I was taken at clear or broad daylight taken at knife point and raped. I can tell anyone how housing has not provided any security, the've only provided us with security when a crime or when a person has been violated.

> I really enjoy doing this project about my neighborhood. This is the first time I write the letter to a American friend, and I have found that it has a lot fun. Before I wrote the first letter, I was kind of scared, because I was afraid if my partner would like my letter and would think that the things I wrote was stupid. However, after I received her letter I was very happy, because she likes my letter and she even told me that she enjoyed reading it so much. From the letter she wrote to me, I can tell that she is a nice person.

> Since I came to America, I have been trying to get to know some American friends. I have found that it's not easy to get along with someone who does not speak your language. When I was in Parsons (My previous school) there was a nice American girl in my class. She helped me when I don't understand about my homework and sometimes she talked to me a lot. However, every time when she talked to me, I was always a listener. The reason that I didn't talk to her that much was because I was afraid if I say something that she couldn't understand. So I don't talk too much in front of American friends. But I do talk much with Japanese or Korean. I don't know why—maybe I feel more comfortable to talk to a person who does not speak English well. Professor Blitz, would you please give me your opinion? Do you think I'm a strange person?

I told her no, she isn't strange. What do you think of these pieces, Mark?

Michael

———————————

Michael:

These are provocative writings. Actually, the first one is pretty scary in its implied—or not so implied—anti-Semitism. I can't really tell just what the student is actually saying. Which Jews is he so mad at? People who live around Mt. Sinai Hospital or Jewish doctors or hospital administrators? I can't tell. It's hard to enter into a constructive conversation with hate expressed so imprecisely.

The second student, who was raped in her neighborhood: what to say? It is just so hard to fathom the number of students who have been the victims of violence. Their ability to carry on is absolutely awe-inspiring. What is this student asking for, after all, but a little security? Even that modicum of a sane life is denied her—how to understand that which is outrageous beyond belief?

Something in this project has made it possible for our students to articulate some of the most important questions—and so directly. I think it is the sharing of information, of making a picture of where we come from for someone else that has led to this moment where the third student is asking about who they are. Do you remember that my students wondered at the beginning of the project about whether the project was about their neighborhoods or about *them*? Maybe they sensed something right from the very beginning about the connection between community and individual, that the two are finally inseparable. The third student's question to you is just so honest. I am sure you supported her with the words she needed, words that were also just.

You could not have sent these excerpts to me at a better time. I say that because, I have to admit, I have been feeling low lately as I have been doubting the value of the Neighborhood Project. I just am not seeing the kind of commitment to the making of this book that I would like. I can't speak for your class, of course, but my students are, as far as I can see, putting the hard work of writing the book off. Too many of them seem to be waiting for someone else in the class to do the work of the book for them. Yes, they have done some fine field research in their neighborhoods and towns, but the time is already past that they should have begun writing their findings up. At this rate they will not leave themselves enough time to get response and revise their work—I dread the idea of publishing first draft work!

Having said all of that, the excerpts you sent me from your students' research notebooks remind me how significant the project is (despite the momentary lull I am now witnessing). It occurs to me, after reading the second and third excerpts, that this project makes available to our students certain avenues, such as, I now see, the notebooks, as well as the correspondences, for dispelling or revising their own sense of being strange. The project requires interactions with others, sometimes even confrontations (I am thinking about Raymond and Angela). It requires weighing one another's perspectives on living, on being a member of a community or, for confronting one's own sense, in the case of your third student, of being an outsider. The project is a powerful lesson in community membership: how does one address someone else whose views conflict quite plainly with one's own? Since our students understand themselves to be part of a hypothetical "community"—at least for the semester—how are they to respond to another community member whose views irritate them to a point where normally they might turn away or undermine such a member's presence in the community? Then, of course, there is the question of how the students relate to us and we to them. I imagine that responding to the first student was difficult.

OK, some good and honest things are coming out of this project. I'll try to maintain this high.

Mark

Michael:

I can't help it. I just met with my students and I am really angry. On too many days my students come to class to meet in their groups and have no new research done. They sit there with blank expressions or grin at me. On too many days they are saying, "We don't know what to do" (no matter how many times I explain or remind them about what they should be doing). On too many days they meet with their groups and admit that they "did not have time to write for the book" or "did not have film to take pictures of that neighborhood" or "forgot to work on the art work for our chapter" or "could not reach the person they were going to interview." When I ask why, there are excuses—always more and more excuses, and many of them are legitimate enough (I am taking six classes and working two jobs and I am sick). Still, even as they make these excuses, they get further behind, closer to our publishing deadlines, but no closer to a product.

Mark

Mark:

The rough drafts of the Eng 102 pieces have come in and they look somewhat ghastly. Our students really need more than a semester to get sufficiently unglued to glue things together in ways that don't feel so wobbly. We are contenting ourselves with very short pieces—3–5 pages plus references, which reflect several-source research and collective thinking across the writings. Looks like there will be five chapters each of which will contain anywhere from 2 to 6 short writings (plus other stuff). In a couple of chapters there will be collaboratively written work. The group doing the Design of a New Community is writing a group introduction to that chapter—sort of an abstract. Joe has submitted a few cover images. So, we are getting "there" without a very clear sense of where "there" is.

Michael

Were we working from expectations that our students could never fulfill? Worse, did our students sense this? Did we have so much of ourselves invested in this project and its success that we pushed too hard toward our conception of perfection, whatever *that* was? Toward students producing the book that we would have? Whatever the classroom dynamics, we were, like our students, growing more tired and sick, and sick and tired, as the semester ground on.

Students began to bicker with each other as they felt they had let their group members down. Students began to complain about each other. Their teachers complained to each other. The semester quickly turned into one of "those" semesters: the bad kind, where teachers and students both wonder why they are doing this. The books simply were not progressing. The students did not, however, entirely give up on each other. They developed a new plan: to publish their books together under one cover, back to back. In other words, at the end of the IUP book, readers would flip the text over and find the John Jay book—or vice versa. Each book would have its own cover, own design, own contents, but each would be the equal of the other.

Mark:

I don't have high hopes for my students having prepared much to send off to your class to review. They don't even seem to have the book cover in hand. I read a few more rough drafts and they are so facile, so flimsy, so much the kinds of things you and I have claimed teachers need more patience for, and I find myself thinking like a conservative: is it too bloody much to ask that students in a second or third semester writing course—college level and part of the core—be able to read a book, write a paragraph, think about what they've just written, read over a piece of writing and notice anything at all about it that needs revision? Am I being a mean bastard, blaming the victim? Isn't there ANY responsibility in the hands of the learners themselves? So many of my students in 102 seem to be floating in a soup of obliviousness and who am I to fish them out and tell them they seem way too close to being hopelessly lost?

Yes, I know they are the ones we need to help, but I feel like I am spinning wheels I've reinvented.

Nearly 13 weeks into the semester and one student "discovers" that she has really done virtually no research—that opinions aren't sufficient, that the stuff I've been saying all semester isn't a lie; another student writes editorials into every paragraph despite her group's VERY strong advice to the contrary, and when she is shown what's what, she smiles and says, more or less, "Whoops." Yet another student has realized that he has lost his research notebook but tells me it's okay, that he hasn't written anything in it anyway. One young man has been enjoying himself all semester, pleased to have an interesting English class, occasionally answering questions, and now I see that he is almost nowhere—should I have seen this? Yes, I suppose I should have known about all their progress, but I've allowed them to be independent, not to be such a watch dog because I'm not a watch dog, and because they are adults—I should not have to supervise all of their homework, but I obviously messed up. I obviously *do* have to bore my way into their homes and projects and everyday lives in ways I can't imagine and invent ways for them to do work that, despite my good wishes for them to have an experience they can do more than hang a manila folder on, so many of them are as lost as they would have been if I had lectured them on the American Psychological Association method of documentation. I'm discouraged. The kids aren't bad, Mark; they're well-intentioned, generally sweet and earnest, but right now I don't feel up to answering this calling, and the ringing is incessant.

I am losing sleep over this project, but I know it's something more than the project. The drafts that I've seen, the fragments, the notes—they all depict city life in a way that only hints at the throb of everyday tension. I wouldn't want anyone who reads the book our students produce to lose sight of the fact that my students have absorbed so much violence, so little peace, that it's a miracle they can find the hope and enthusiasm to even try to imagine a better neighborhood. At the same time, I want my students to experience the rigor of serious, careful writing and revising, editing, and proofreading. I want them to care about this document they are supposed to be producing. And they do care. As I've worked side by side with them, looking over their shoulders as they met in their editorial groups, discussing the process with them, showing them alternatives to some of the ways they have been composing their essays and chapters, I've somehow missed how unsettling the whole project can be to them. Even as they smile through a conversation about the problems in their particular neighborhood or on their streets, they are being asked to face the reality of how strained their everyday lives are. I am losing sleep, but more troubling to me is how easy it is to lose sight of the possible connections between a project like this one and the day to day movements our students choreograph in the midst of chaos.

In fact, I can't seem to help *anyone* sleep better, Mark. Maybe my students don't need to write essays about neighborhoods; maybe they just need a good night's sleep away from the fears of gunfire and poverty, of children-snatchers and drug-dealers, of rogue-cops and arsonists stealing the lives out from entire city-blocks. They need a day of safety from rotten, festering spouses who see everyone as an enemy and loved ones most of all, a single night of rest from the bombardment by ubiquitous sources of derision that they do not, yet, hold the American dream in their hands, that they will never hold it, nor the few dollars it takes to forget the dream long enough to catch their breath, that they cannot guarantee their own kids a better life than this overly compli-cated, desiccated one that saturates the brown bricks of overstuffed, underfed housing projects. They need to sleep a sleep that's not the unconsciousness of exhaustion from having worked too many hours and then gone to school after rearranging frayed strands of child-care with already exhausted family or friends or centers who offer too little supervision and too much television to babies who will know their parents by their half-open eyes. They need something I can't give them, Mark—and the problem is that I want to give it, and they want to get it, and sometimes we all get fooled into thinking it's something anyone else has got.

Michael

Somehow the book happened.[6] We say it this way because the "steps" leading toward the completed project felt more like spasms than orderly movements toward a collective goal. Our classrooms, for the final four or five sessions of the course, were studies in frenetic, and frantic, effort. We held impromptu grammar lessons; students met in small groups and nit-picked their way through single paragraphs before their teacher had to come over and remind them of the larger problems that still needed their attention. Group leaders shook up their colleagues with reminders that this project was supposed to be "collaborative"; too many were not producing their fair share. Papers flew around the room. Students used the blackboards for listing tasks still to be done. Someone's tape recorder played an interview with a neighborhood know-it-all and a half-dozen students yelled over to the tape's owner, "Turn that thing down!" Stu-dents approached us with very professional questions about layout, cover design, tables of contents. We kept extra office hours in which to meet individually with students having problems with topic paragraphs, quotations, citations, even punctuation. We sat in on groups, read copy, made comments, asked questions. Students were genuinely curious about ways to vary the organization within a particular piece of writing so it wouldn't be "boring." One John Jay student stood up in the midst of a noisy workshop and announced that he was going to read his chap-ter out loud. The rest of the class shouted him down and demanded that Michael keep him quiet so they could work! Mark's students debated loudly over which photographs were good enough to scan into the com-puter for inclusion. Out of nowhere, some students wanted to know if their chapters dealt sufficiently with "comparison and contrast," "description," and "analogy." One student begged to be allowed to run back to the library for fear that she "might have" plagiarized a "couple of pages" from one of her sources. (She was allowed to go!)

The deadline drew closer; final evaluations loomed; the John Jay students were worried that the IUP students were smarter and better writers; the IUP students complained that their John Jay partners were probably ahead of them; the copy centers might need more lead time than we could give them; we were never going to get everything done.

And the fact is, when up against deadlines and with a sense of urgency that became a sort of purpose of its own, students produced texts. The effort they made in the last two weeks of the semester may very well have equaled their previous thirteen weeks of work combined. By semester's end, our students had indeed made something unique. In which aspects of this mad rush did we, as composition teachers, play signficant roles? Did we teach writing? Composing? Editing? Community-building? Collaborative research? We would have to argue that we did all of the above, but we would quickly add that it might be more accurate to say we helped create environments in which this kind of intensive learning could happen. We played the roles of lecturer, facilitator, coach, cheerleader, resource, parental figure, assistant copyeditor, critic. Sometimes we allowed disorder to reign; sometimes we had to rein in the (potential) terror. About the overall experience of teaching composition, James Sledd has said, "Our enterprise . . . remains as various, as strange, as vexing, as absorbing, as people are. . . . The final importance of our work, if we can keep from freezing in the snowstorm of student papers, is that in our petty way we cannot help dramatizing the essentiality of the free maker" (104). We are not so sure that we would concur with Sledd that composition teachers are, generally, "petty" about presenting students' works. But we do agree that the teaching of writing is a strange business that puts us in the position of witnessing the dramatic *making* that our students can and do.

The 190-page book ended up having two titles to reflect its two halves: IUP's *A Better Neighborhood: Coming Together* and JJC's *Where Is Utopia?: Focusing on Our Neighborhoods*. The book features descriptions of neighborhoods, interviews, photographs, and researched essays on how neighborhoods are created, about the architecture, neighborhood demographics, crime, pollution, aesthetics, recreation, transportation, and designs for the kinds of neighborhoods in which our students would like to live.

The research consisted mostly of traditional library sources, which turned out to be a problem. Since the students had agreed to incorporate and cite their library findings, much of their work read a little like book reports, consisting primarily of abstractions or generalities such as, "There are many types of neighborhoods in the United States." We do not mean to suggest that library research, in and of itself, was insignificant, but as many research-writing teachers have discovered, a problem occurs when library research is reported for the sake of the reporting, rather than to support critical thought or as a context for the construction of creative insights. Indeed, in the first chapter to the IUP half of the book, which was supposed to define the concept of neighborhoods and describe local neighborhoods, the students did little more than quote sources and list a series of short quotes from themselves about their neighborhoods. There was little analysis of their research. In fact, throughout both halves of the book, the students did not go much beyond the act of presentation. Even when the students' research would turn up powerful texts or information, they would do little with that information. One student reported the following from a "friend":

> "I bought a pistol almost a year ago. When I'm driving around in my car and I have my gun I feel invincible. Who is gonna beat a gun? Hell, once someone even sees it, their gonna change their mind. If I'm driving by myself and a car load of guys whips me the finger, I turn around and chase them. The way I see it 'Fuck them I have a gun.'"

The student reported these words in a chapter on neighborhood crime, but then did nothing with it: no questioning of the friend's words, action, or attitude. In addition, in a chapter supposed to explore solutions to problems in neighborhoods, the students mainly presented media–like generalities: complaints about violence on TV, calls for welfare, health care, and education reform.

The problem, as we see it, is that, for the most part, the students did not make connections between the insights they created about their own lives during the letter writing in the first half of the semester and their research reported in the book. For instance, one of the neighborhood problems the IUP students focused on was alcohol abuse. Next to a photo of a beer distributor near the IUP campus, they wrote: "Every week, Indiana beer distributors are stormed by college students. DUIs, public drunkenness and crime result from the abuse of alcohol." But even as the students wrote this, they did not connect it to themselves. Their words sounded as if the problem of alcohol abuse belonged to a place called "IUP," not to the students who attend IUP, a position hard to defend after the work of the first half of the semester. It was as if, and we can say this about large portions of both halves of the book, they wrote as though they were not *in* the neighborhoods about which they wrote. One IUP student wrote: "One night in the beginning of June of this year,

I got a phone call from a friend that I have known for many years. She called to tell me that her parents were in jail, they were arrested for selling drugs. Soon after their car was impounded, and maybe the house too." This, surely is a powerful revelation, but it is presented as a "set-up" for several pages of disconnected thoughts about crime that end, "As, you can see there are problems every where you go. It is a part of life and will always exist."

The JJC half of the book also included significant personal truths. One student wrote, "I interviewed a girl who wants to conceil her identity, and who is recently in East New York (Brooklyn). So I will call her Susan. Susan had a brother who was fourteen years old. He was shot on the chest by a teenager his own age." Here was a powerful truth. The writer connected this information to violent crime statistics and then drew the conclusion that "Teenagers are not safe in our neighborhoods." But that's as far as it went. Even when students wrote about those issues that directly affected them—crime, economic problems, violence, boredom, as well as the deterioration of neighborhoods—their analyses typically consisted of single sentences which seemed intended to close discussion of complicated issues.

The JJC students were able to imbue their half of the book with a sense of the history behind some of the places they live. They included significant reports of the development of their boroughs and neighborhoods, such as the Bronx and Rosedale, Queens. Still, they did little with this history. Even when the students dealt with the histories of individuals, with the personal impact of, say, moving from one neighborhood to another, the subject is reported as if they have little or no connection to it: "Whether or not one is ready to move from one neighborhood to another, they must be able to prepare their family and themselves for the emotional and psychological changes."

Of course both halves of the book had strengths. Throughout both, interesting bits of interviews are present: neighbors, people on the street, police, city officials, religious leaders. Among the more startling of these moments was a chapter in the IUP half, Chapter IV: "Pictures of People Being Interviewed." Here the students included photographs of people in their lives or people they met randomly on the streets of Indiana along with a quote from each of them about small town life. Most of these interviewees extol the virtues of small town life: "I like the neighborhood I live in, it's very nice. . . . My neighborhood has a mix of young people, children, and older adults. I think that is a good learning experience." But some are startling for a different kind of honesty, like this from a seventeen-year-old African American citizen of Indiana, PA: "This town sucks. It is for the white man. I need city life. Indiana is a racist poor hick town. (If I am not dead by 20, I will be getting out of here.)" In a sense, the IUP students created in this chapter a powerful gallery of people and comments, but the larger context of the book as a whole does not sufficiently suggest that this is how these photos and quotations should be read. Instead, the "gallery" is presented in a book dedicated largely to reports, with no connection made between the living people presented in this chapter and the words culled from their reading.

There were significant moments of discovery in the making of the JJC book. For example, one group, studying their housing project, agreed that the absence of working streetlamps contributed to the high rate of violent crime and drug traffic. The obvious "fix," then, would be to replace the bulbs in the streetlamps. But they discovered that the city had given up on these replacements because they lasted, according to one city official, less than twenty-four hours before being broken (by rocks or bullets). The students suggested that metal cages be placed over the bulbs but were told that nothing would work and that, besides, that was too expensive. These students noted that other neighborhoods had working streetlamps, some even with wire cages! They concluded that a housing project was "doomed" to stay an area of violent crime by its very design. And in a chapter about designing future neighborhoods, the students articulated the complexity of laws and concerns that go into urban planning and infrastructure design and maintenance. At the same time, despite all the complexity, the students remained committed to the idea that better living conditions are possible for us all: "Neighbors really are the most important component in the community, and people do have to cooperate with each other in order to create a better neighborhood." Also, the JJC students included an "About the Authors" section that speaks of their hope. Many of them name their desires, not only to get their education, but to become computer programmers, law enforcement officials, and lawyers: people dedicated to making better lives for themselves and others.

We recognize that our students produced a significant artifact which represents a shared concern for life. Both halves demonstrate an attempt to accomplish a significant feat, to point to better and healthier living, and all in a semester. Each suggests that one of the best hopes for our neighborhoods is for the people in them to come together to work for their health. They suggest establishing Neighborhood Crime Watches or forming discussion and action groups. We cannot help but read such suggestions from our students as a reminder of the obvious value of the human connection of the Interstate Neighborhood project. We wondered, however, if the project, and if *we*, had done enough to encourage the deep study of lived experience our students had set out to examine.

And now, how would we grade these efforts?

Michael:

I decided to give my class a B+ for their book. I met with them today as a class and explained that I appreciated the work they did and the level of achievement they reached. But I also told them that I did not believe that they had reached an A in terms of quality or effort. I explained that as much as they did, that I did not feel they worked hard enough. They procrastinated. They did not listen to the suggestions and strategies I made available to them, ideas that would have made their work more effective. And the individual groups did not work together as they could have to make the different chapters of the book work together as a whole. Yes, there were parts of the book that were significant, but I also reminded them that there were still parts of the book that were unfinished (they did not even include the poetry/lyrics and artwork sections that their table of contents promises!) or that needed more revision. Of course, they were disappointed that they did not get an A for their book, but they also realized, I think, the validity of what I was saying.

Mark

Mark:

For many of the reasons you mentioned in your note, I gave my students a grade of B for the book. They wanted to know what you'd given your students, but at the time, I hadn't heard. My students were a bit disappointed, especially those who had done the finest work. But as a class, they agreed that the finished book had *lots* of problems—typos, grammatical errors, weak essays, less-than-spectacular use of source materials including their partners' letters. I pointed out that there had been ample time to do all sorts of revisions and consultation with each other and with me; they had not made the best use of most of their time, and they conceded that point, as well. I did not have the impression that their agreement about the grade was prompted by any sort of desire to give the teacher what he wants. Rather, we spoke quite candidly about the difference between the best of intentions ("the best laid plans") and the ways in which any of us carry out those intentions.

Michael

At the same time, some of the most important learning probably could not be measured in the written product of a book on neighborhoods. As one student wrote, "The project taught me about being selfish. I wanted things [how the book was organized] my own way. This would be all right if I lived in the middle of nowhere by myself, but I live among many other people." The fact is that both the book and the letter-writing projects had profound impact on some of our students. As one IUP student wrote with regard to her New York City partner's letters: "It just blew my mind to even be able to imagine being 20 years old, mother of two children (one four year old and one four month old), going to college, working part time, and living alone with no husband or boyfriend, no parents, just children that you are completely responsible for."

Throughout the course of the project we saw a slow but notable loosening of some very tight constraints on our students' inclinations to open up. Or, to put it more directly, our students enjoyed the possibility of candor. They liked the idea that they could be themselves in their writing and that being themselves was relevant to academic work. This was a new experience for them in the academy and, for many, in their lives. They wondered if it was possible to like—or dislike—people they had never met. They considered the implications of trying to design a community which would have to accommodate people whose lives they could barely fathom. Most significant was our students' expressed surprise that correspondence, that asking questions, constitutes research. It had never dawned on them that they had been conducting research all their lives. And it was amazing to them that people from "far away" might be interested in their observations, their philosophies, their forays into understanding their own world. The effects of this correspondence were often profound. After Raymond received Angela's "blunt" response to what she identified as his negativity, he not only struggled to regain his confidence, he actually began to do far more serious work and to become a more committed student as evidenced by subsequent academic successes. Angela, who had said in a later letter to Raymond that she'd not taken her education that seriously until taking the research-writing course, did, in fact, go on to be accepted to law school. Finally, one of Michael's students stopped her class cold one day when she said, "Until now, I didn't even know I lived anywhere. I mean, it's like I wasn't anywhere. Now I think about it and I see this place I live in and the place I go to school in. And I could see why some places fall apart. The people in them don't even know they're there."

Notes

1. Our students have limited access to the Internet, so we had to employ other means for connecting our classes, such as the mail. As we prepare this book, more and more of Mark's students are finding e-mail access. The situation is not changing, however, as quickly for Michael's students.

2. While IUP has some seventy-nine buildings (for approximately 13,000 undergraduates), John Jay has two buildings (for approximately 10,500 undergraduates).

3. While we both assigned the task of keeping research notebooks, the assignment only "worked" for Michael's students. Part of the problem is that Mark could not find enough class time to make the notebooks an integral part of each class period's activities. The students consequently began to see the notebooks as extraneous, as busy work. Michael was able to incorporate the notebooks as a central class activity. Not surprisingly, his students responded accordingly.

4. We include excerpts, rather than whole letters, from our students' neighborhood project correspondence. We do not employ ellipses to mark elisions, except where using an ellipsis will maintain meaning. We have chosen this way of presenting the students' writing in order to create a "smoother," more coherent reading experience, and also because we are more interested in creating a documentary about the Interstate Neighborhood Project than we are in providing an ethnographic transcription of it (Ott, Boquet, and Hurlbert).

5. Our students were creating portfolios of their letters to be evaluated.

6. Following are the tables of contents for the two class books.

The IUP book, *Toward a Better Neighborhood: Coming Together*

Chapter IV
1) Pictures of People Being Interviewed
2) Poetry and Lyrics
3) Conclusion

The JJC book: *Where Is Utopia?: Focusing on Neighborhoods*

Introduction
Chapter One: Defining a Neighborhood
The Characteristics of a Neighborhood
Ideas of a Neighborhood
Product of an Environment
Chapter Two: Neighborhood Portraits and Histories
The Bronx: What It Used To Be and What It Is Now
Rosedale, Queens: Then and Now
Far Rockaway: 1690–1920
Chapter Three: Neighborhood Differences
Ready To Move
Relocation Blues
Transportation
Chapter Four: Critical Issues in Neighborhoods
Crime and Its Possibilities for Control
No Other Choice
Violence Among Us
Critical Issues
Drugs & Violence: How They Affect the Youth Within the Neighborhood
Chapter Five: Where Is Utopia
Designing a Neighborhood
Applying the Techniques of Neotraditional Architecture to an Existing Community
A New Existence
Recreation and Entertainment Facilities
Planning and Other Development Functions
That's What Neighbors Are For
Creating a Safe Neighborhood: Infrastructural Design and Layout
About the Authors

Introduction to Part 5

Mark:

Following today's Theme-A Lecture (The Thematic Studies Program's interdisciplinary, team-taught course entitled "The Individual in Conflict"), the four professors met to discuss how the class had gone and what we plan for next week. Somehow the conversation turned to last semester's students (who are with us again for the 2nd half of the Theme-A lecture) and their increasingly personal and, as Don Goodman put it, "often heartbreaking papers." This led us to wonder how to deal with these writings. Don is a sociologist. Geoff Fairweather is a musician, Jerry Markowitz is a historian and is also chair of the Thematic Studies Program, and I'm the English component.

Don added, "They write such moving stuff! I read it, and I don't know what to write back to them, or even *if* I should. I feel like calling them up and saying to them 'yeah—it's tough—life's tough—I'm with you.'" Don had been referring to a paper he'd gotten in which a student in his discussion section had written about "a young man" whose father would come home from work and expect a hot meal on the table, waiting for him. If the meal wasn't hot, or if it was delayed, he'd beat his wife up. If the son intervened or even spoke up, the father would go after him, as well. The student ended the paper wondering what, if anything, would ever change in this situation.

Don said, "As far as I could tell, this paper may well have been about this kid's family, but I don't know! I don't know how to read it! That's the thing! We keep asking for these writings, but I'm beginning to see how difficult it is to respond to these papers."

Geoff said, "They certainly know how to tell the hard truth when they put their minds to it!"

Don asked, "But what do you say? I mean what do you say?" Jerry asked me what I thought, and I said something about not having any prescription for knowing what to say, and that the reason I'm writing *Letters for the Living* is because it's an important question to be struggled with.

Jerry, who's read our prospectus, said, "That's right! Your book is about this . . . well, hurry up with it!"

Michael

5 For the Living

Michael:

I can't stop thinking about our recent phone conversation about the Neighborhood Project. You said, "After all is written and done, these kids still have to go home to the problems they wrote about." When I reread the book our students produced in the Project, I'm still surprised that they don't write much about their feelings about going home, about making new homes in the neighborhoods of their imaginations.

Now I'm thinking about next courses, what I might do with the new groups who will do the next projects. I know I want to think some more about home and living at home, moving away from home, not having a home. About home, Michael. I want to build something new with regard to the idea of the *lives* that are "housed" together each semester. Any thoughts?

Mark

Mark:

When my students and I write, we make things, we build things, we dismantle things, we play, we desire, we resist. A strategy I think may have some value in terms of improving the quality of communications is an attention to physical structures. Because I am also a carpenter, I have spent some time learning about the science of physical structures (for a couple of wonderful books on the subject, I recommend J. E. Gordon's *Structures, or Why Things Don't Fall Down* and *The New Science of Strong Materials*). I tell my students that language operates a lot like structures—there are tensions and compressions, hinges, fractures, stresses and strains. These are not just (extended?) metaphors; they are ways by which language—like walls and arches and spans and beams—succeeds or fails in supporting overall structures, forms, events.

Michael

Michael:

I have been thinking about last weekend: we were side by side at the computer at your place, reading over the draft of Part 4: Letters. When we got to the e-mails that introduce the Interstate Neighborhood Project, you laughed out loud at something I had written in one of my letters to you:

> I never assign readings in my research writing classes—or topics for that matter. This is going to mean quite a change for me—which is good—except that I am also uncomfortable about making any required texts the center of my students' attentions for the semester. Hmmm. It can be worked out though.

Remember that you said that it will sound, for a moment, to some readers, like my classes never do *anything*? Well, maybe so.

Perhaps we should explain in *Letters for the Living* what it is we actually do in our classes as a way of setting a context for how it is that our students come to write some of the extraordinary books they do. I'd also like to talk about how our teaching is, among other things, a form of cultural studies pedagogy in which the study of culture, Multicultural student-centeredness and poetics work to make the heart of a composition class.

A pedagogy combining imagination, craft, and the making of various cultures.

A workshop pedagogy: an organic, creative, socially responsible pedagogy.

Mark

_____

Mark:

I go to school in the morning with the idea, with the anticipation, that I am going to have a chance to listen to students talk about what they're working on, to read aloud to my students and be read to *by* them. And once in a while (maybe more often than I realize), I present them with a few ideas about ways to approach writing or revising or even reading that they hadn't thought of before.

It's a strange business, I grant you. Whenever I tell students that they will become better writers when they write more often and more stuff, they smile at me. They think I'm slightly daffy in my circular reasoning. But by semester's end, throughout all these years, my students discover that they have created a substantial body of writing and that the later pieces truly are more sophisticated, more insightful, more imaginative, and yes, more competently done than the works they'd produced earlier in the term. They will have written letters, reviews, maybe a speech, a pamphlet, often a booklet. They will have written one or more pieces in collaboration with others. And they will have been read—widely. They will have done research, and they will have been "made to" search for meaning in each other's writings. They will have filled a notebook (or two), and they will have written notes in the margins of their colleagues' notebooks. For the brief time we spend together, a few hours each week in a classroom, my students *are* writers. We treat each other as writers, we talk about the world as writers, we read books and poems, even body language as writers.

Sometimes, much to my own surprise, students in my "developmental" writing classes do exceptionally well on the departmental exit exams, as do my first-year writing classes. I say I am always surprised because I do not pay attention to these exams during the semester. I assure my students that the exams will be a far easier piece of business than anything they are going to do during the semester, and inevitably, around 75% or more of the students pass these exams (the departmental average has always been around 55%). I don't know whether it would be fair to say that *all* of my students should pass. Some of them arrive at JJC after having had far too little high school preparation for any kind of advanced work (though I don't hesitate to add that it is patently unfair to blame those excellent high school teachers out there who are doing their best against all odds). But the fact is, the vast majority of my students come away from the semester with a sense of competence and confidence that reading and writing are not simply the dreary business of school, but a potentially integral part of their lives, a part that they can shape, craft, control, and yes, enjoy.

It wouldn't be far off to say that my writing pedagogy is typified in a class moment in which I suggest to students that working on a particular piece of writing isn't so different from imagining, and then acting upon, a design for a place in which to live, a home. Their ideas, styles, desires, frustrations, recollections, notions of comfort or discomfort are all partly in evidence in the design of their writings. And just as they might do in their ideal homes, they can, in their writings, continually rearrange the furniture not only to their own satisfaction but also in an effort to create an environment that reflects their vision of what a common, inhabitable space can be.

Michael

Michael:

In my classes, I, too, want students to recognize themselves as writers, to carve out spaces in their lives in which thinking of themselves *as* writers will not seem utterly foreign. I want students to come to a point where they are so comfortable in these spaces that they refuse to be evicted by professors, or anyone for that matter, who know nothing about teaching writing or who do not write themselves. So, my students will not write dummy-run exercises. They will learn to improve their writing by experimenting and improvising with their writings, and they will become better readers of their own writing by responding to the writing of their colleagues.

Mark

Mark:

The tone of your last note made me feel like cheerleading, but I also am not sure about what you mean when you say, "they refuse to be evicted by professors." What do you have in mind?

Michael

Michael:

I was thinking about Jed Rasula's *The American Poetry Wax Museum*. Although he's talking about poetry anthologies and the "institutionalization" of poetry, in his first section, he suggests, to me anyway, ways to articulate important questions about the teaching of composition: What does it mean to "adopt" a handbook? a reader? to ask students to write vapid, easily consumable discourse? harmless (that is, changing nothing) writing? In what sense do teachers of writing fulfill what Rasula calls the postmodern "repetition compulsion" when they ask students to create imitations of published writings (9)? To what extent do teachers assign such repetitions in order "to certify" the authority of that with which they are already familiar (10)? What are teachers sponsoring when they assign the new, glossy cultural and Multicultural studies readers? Just what sort of composing are writing teachers teaching; what sort of compositions are their students making?

Mark

Mark:

You echo the questions we have been asking ourselves and each other for years. By now, the questions have a little bit of an edge, don't they?

Sometimes, when I think about trying to articulate my "pedagogy" (I put the word in quotes because sometimes it doesn't sound very "living" to me. It sounds like a word we use at conferences, one that doesn't quite connect to my everyday work.), I have to go back to my own basics. As I've often mentioned, one of the most influential books for me was Postman and Weingartner's *Teaching as a Subversive Activity*. What they saw as "subversive" never struck me as such; rather, their ideas about teaching seemed so fundamental, I can't imagine conducting a class without at least some of their ideas underpinning what I do. In their chapter, "What's Worth Knowing?" they write:

> We have a possibility for you to consider: suppose that you decide to have the entire "curriculum" consist of questions. These questions would have to be worth seeking answers to not only from your point of view

but, more importantly, from the point of view of the students. In order to get still closer to reality, add the requirement that the questions must help the students develop and internalize concepts that will help them to survive in the rapidly changing world of the present and future. (59)

They go on to supply a list of their own questions. First they say,

> Even the most sensitive teacher cannot always project himself into the perspective of his students, and he dare not assume that *his* perception of reality is necessarily shared by them. With this limitation in mind, we can justify the list we will submit on several grounds. First, many of these questions *have* literally been asked by children and adolescents when they were permitted to respond freely to the challenge of "What's Worth Knowing?" Second, some of these questions are based on our careful *listening* to students, even though they were not at the time asking questions. (60)

And the questions they offer have always struck me as dead-on:

> "What do you worry about most?"

> "If you had an important idea that you wanted to let everyone (in the world) know about, how might you go about letting them know?"

> "What, if anything, seems to you to be worth dying for? How did you come to believe this? What seems worth living for?"

> "What's a 'good idea'?" (62-65)

And so on. By the way, one of their coolest questions is: "Who do you think has the most important things to say today? To whom? How? Why?" (65).

Our students ask some pretty cool questions, too: "Why do we have to write? Why do we have to spend so much time worrying about this stuff?"

I always assure them that they *don't* have to. But (quickly) I add that there are some very good reasons to see themselves as writers and to become active writers. They expect I'll talk about jobs and corporate requirements, graduate school work, and so on, and certainly I mention these things as real factors that will have some bearing on students' futures. But I also talk about the idea of the social whole, of being social beings. And I keep, in my own mind, Postman and Weingartner's remarks on the importance of shared perceptions:

> Since our perceptions come from us and our past experience, it is obvious that each individual will perceive what is "out there" in a unique way. We have no common world, and communication is possible only to the extent that two perceivers have similar purposes, assumptions, and experience. The process of becoming an effective social being is contingent upon seeing the other's point of view. (90)

Obviously, working closely together as writers and readers whose work will focus on issues and matters we consider to be important (or, as you suggest with your students, things we are "burning to tell the world") will allow us at least to begin to see things from each other's point of view. It is a start toward finding, or making, a "common world."

Michael

Michael:

I have been thinking, as I often do when I sit in a class in the middle of all this creativity, that I am the luckiest person in the world. I love when we have whole class discussions and there is a balance of serious, thought-expanding talk—and laughter. I love to listen as my students share plans and inspirations for the formal experiments they are making in their books.

Michael, I think that composition studies needs to develop, further, the idea and role of the "workshop." Remember when I wrote to you once, after one of your poetry readings at Biblio's, and I was wondering out loud about the fact that we ever forget the power of poetry to remake experience, to remake ourselves? Well, I have always wondered why composition people have not borrowed more of a sense of the creative and imaginative potential of poetics in the making of their classes. I think that composition teachers should consider what can be learned from creative writing workshops and pedagogy. Now I am not talking about designing the master-writer-with-neophytes-at-the-feet workshops, or workshops where students compete to outshine their peers in their master's eyes. I am talking about the making of safe communities—to the extent that we are able—where people explore what they need to write—where they learn the power of craft and the imagination.

Here's some sketching out of what I have in mind:

> The making of workshops beyond the limitations of traditional, creative writing workshops, which Wendy Bishop has described as "pedagogically static" and "conservative" of teacher-centered instruction (12). The workshop should be about what students need to write, not what teachers want to hear.

> Workshop: but with Derek Owens' commitment to searching for the poetic work that students may do. Here I am thinking of his call for classes where students explore varieties of discourse and discursive experience, rather than monoliths, such as the compare and contrast paper.

> Workshop: but with the poetic innovation and rhetorical responsibility of something akin to June Jordan's vision of *Poetry for the People* (Muller). Here students discuss their writing in relation to political and social realities (such as who gets published and read and who doesn't and

why. Here students take their writing to the community doing public readings or through self-publication).

Composition studies must also reflect a greater awareness of, and interest in, Multicultural studies in connection to composing. And here I don't mean teaching writing so that different people write the same, sound the same. Our students come from different places with different experiences, but we can set our classrooms up in such a way that no one point of origin is valorized over another—no one discursive journey, no one discursive destination. Instead, students can explore varieties of composing processes, not to mention variety of end results. Just this semester I had a meeting with an earnest student of European American descent. She was making suggestions for revision on the text of an African American student whose book, about life in her Philadelphia neighborhood, was appropriately written in Black English. The white student was "correcting" the book's English, making it consistent with the rules of what she perceived to be Standard English. When I pointed out to her that in her desire to help she was perhaps violating this text, she said, "Do you mean that by correcting this writing I am making mistakes?" I said, "Yes." "Do you mean to say that all of my years of learning grammar was not enough?" I said, "Yes." She was frustrated, but she was learning.

So why study our students' differences and stories? I think we say it to each other all the time: to help students better understand their experiences in relation to their cultures and to work toward solutions to the problems they face everyday. This is composition as culture building: composing to understand one's life and the lives of others, even to try to better the world.

Mark

Mark:

If someone were to ask you, "How do your writing courses work?", how would you respond? I'm asking this because a couple of colleagues and I were preparing for a course we will team-teach next semester, and one asked me, "So, what are you *doing* in your writing class these days?" I described some of the work my students are doing, and I told her about the impending student book projects. She said, "Sounds neat, but what do you *do* in the *class*? How does your course *work*?" I described, more or less, what I do from day to day, which is pretty much what you do, as well. But I felt I wasn't accurately portraying the composition class.

How would you answer?

Michael

Michael:

It's an intriguing question. Not because we haven't thought about these things, but because I haven't made myself step "out" of the class in a long time in order to do this kind of ethnographic observation.

Let's see. At the beginning of each semester, I ask students to write a short book about something they are "burning to tell the world."[1] My aim, here, is to provide an opportunity for my students to create something with staying power: something not for consumption and disposal, rather an artifact, art work, something that develops over time, offering opportunities for metacritical work. Along the way, my students also learn about fluency, architecture, chronology, the intricacies of narrative, maintaining tone, coherence, and cohesion.

Some students create the minimum twenty-page books. Some inevitably do less, but some create books as long as sixty pages, depending on the topic and its needs. For example, one student wrote a book about her work with "problem" children; another wrote about life in an inner city Catholic school in Philadelphia. Both of these books were over fifty pages of text. One wrote about remembering high school days and friends (her book had photos as well as text), while one of her classmates wrote his book as a reminiscence on one season of a central PA high school baseball team. These latter books were shorter—around thirty pages each—as was another book about one woman's experience of working on a male-dominated job in a boathouse.

We always discuss these options and formats in class, so I guess part of what "goes on" in my class is a lot of whole-group planning and brainstorming and collaborative inspiration-making. I always bring copies of past books to this opening class to let my students look them over. When students write their own books, they bring drafts to class for their peers' responses. And as the project deadline draws near, students meet in groups in the class to share ideas about the final "look" for the books. Then they desktop publish their work.

I'm not sure I'm actually answering your colleague's question yet. But this is useful for me to think about. What do *you* say?

Mark

Mark:

It's strange that when I look over my syllabi for composition classes, I find that they don't give much of a sense of the kinds of activities my students and I engage in during the semester. Maybe these attempts at description are coming at a good time for us. I *do* want to know how our writing courses work. My students write books, too, but to get them to that point, there *is* a process, and that's the day to day work.

I assign frequent short writings early in my composition classes. These first pieces are designed to help students build a writing portfolio. Each of these compositions must be approximately two pages long and must take up something students have learned during that week. For example, as part of the second or third class, I take my students for a walk around the block. As you know, four blocks around New York City can be a field trip in themselves. We look around, we talk about the immediate neighborhood, the buildings, the streets, the people, cars, sounds, smells, anything we choose. Of course students bring their notebooks. When we get back to class, everyone writes for ten minutes or so, sometimes simply organizing the notes they took, sometimes coming up with a catchy opening line or two relating to the walk. Then we get into a "circle" (actually more of an amoebae shape) and talk for a few minutes about what we saw, heard, felt, remembered, and so on. Some students may read aloud from what they wrote.

The assignment is then to write a narrative or a travel-log, an editorial or an excellent personal letter (or letter to the editor) about something they learned about themselves or the city during the walk. (On one of these occasions, "Neil" began his composition, memorably: "If I say I took a walk around the block, I'd be lying. I rolled around the block in my wheelchair. But in a way, I did take a walk. I was thinking that walking around a city block in Manhattan isn't always easier than pushing yourself around on wheels.")

So, this is something I *do* in my class.

Michael

_____

Michael:

I really like the idea of the (very) local "field trip." I bet I could do similar things on the IUP campus or around it. One of the things I like about that activity is that it begins in the ordinary but allows students to see, and to make, something potentially extraordinary.

But I want to talk some more about the ordinary. It sounds pretty flashy, probably, that our students write books and complete elaborate, collaborative projects. But, as you said, there's a process (a madness to our method?) *and* a routine that, like it or not, is as important to my classes as the high-profile end results.

I'm going to describe, if I can, what my students do for the typical second-half of the semester, and I'll start at the end. They produce a class book. The book is a study or series of studies and/or responses to the individually produced books from the first half of the course. The idea here is to give students the opportunity to have the experience of being read carefully and to help the students see the effects that their (prior) writings can have by examining the responses of their colleagues. The class book also gives students a chance to design strategies and offer solutions to social problems presented in the individual books. The pieces in the class book may be written individually or collaboratively, depending on the decision of the writers, the class, and an editorial panel elected by the students. All of the students in the class receive the same grade for the book (unless I have a compelling reason to grade someone individually, as I did on at least one occasion when a student never did any work and didn't show up to class most of the time).

Now, how do we get to this endpoint? That's the nitty gritty that seems hardest to write about because, quite frankly, the narrative can't possibly be as interesting as the daily work often is. Students must photocopy drafts of their work in advance of the class period in which we will discuss their work. So if "Bob" is going to have his work discussed on Thursday, he must distribute it on Tuesday. (For each class period, at least four students will have their work discussed in detail.) On Thursday, then, the class sits in a circle, and we go around, each student saying one thing they like or think is working in Bob's draft. Then we go around the circle again, this time each student making a suggestion for revision. During this activity, Bob doesn't speak. Instead, Bob takes notes on what he hears (which really does work in helping students learn how to listen and attend carefully and non-defensively). At the end of the workshop, Bob may answer any question or make any comment he wishes. To help keep the atmosphere non-aggressive, all suggestions for revision must be made in the form of a question. For example, on her turn, "Alice" might ask, "How would it change the meaning of your introduction if you explained *why* you were so mad at your father?" Bob would then, if he chooses, write that question down and, again if he wishes, answer it when his turn came to speak.

By the way, each student maintains a Response Portfolio that is a record of their responding to the writing of their peers in this class. In it, students put: 1) a photocopy of every workshop paper to which they have responded and 2) copies of their own workshop writing with their colleagues' comments. When I meet with students to offer suggestions for how they might become better responders, any notes students may take during these meetings also go into the Response Portfolio.

When I'm lucky enough to teach composition in a computer classroom, the students also write at their work stations, but they also move around to read and respond to each other's work or to meet with collaborators to discuss further writing plans. If I can, I try to arrange some form of public reading from their class writings. I arrange for a room, students bring refreshments, they invite friends or relatives to come. And I have, on more than one occasion, told them at these moments, "Look what you've done. As a group of people, you are larger than some western Pennsylvanian towns, but among other things, you have written a book together."

OK. I think I'm saying that what I do in a writing class is to try to arrange for the most absorbing, collaborative, supportive intellectual environment for writers that I can. I'm also saying that my students spend their fifteen weeks with me *as writers* whose work will add up to something lasting.

Mark

Mark:

Work. I confess I love that word. My students find that amusing. But when I explain to them why I think the word is so rich, I think they begin to understand. Yes, we—students and teachers—work hard in our writing classes. But we also do good works. We make things that work—sometimes well, sometimes not so well. We can work on a piece of writing; we can give something or someone "the works"; we can throw a wrench in, or smooth out the "works." I tell my students that they are working all the time, that their bodies are working, that their consciousness and unconscious are hard at work, that they are converting energy to work, that *living* is a form of work, and so on. By the time I tell them that they will be working together to produce substantial "bodies" of work, they want me to spell it out: specifically what work will they be expected to do each time they meet with me and each time they are doing homework.

I guess this is what's at the heart of the question, "What do you *do* in your class?" The answer depends a lot on the teacher's, and the students', conception of work. Here are some more things we do, and how we do them:

Usually in the third week of the writing course, we go to the library to do some "treasure hunting." Students can simply browse around until they find something of interest. In their notebooks, they write one page describing what they've found and making a note about how they found it. I generally ask students to try to find at least three such "treasures." Obviously, such an experience helps to familiarize students with the library itself. More importantly, it suggests to students that their own interests are broader than they might suppose.

As for the day-to-day workshop component of the course, it would be interesting to compare our approaches. My writing classes also meet twice a week. Some days I designate as group work days. On these days, I pick three or four names, at random, of students whose drafts will be discussed in the subsequent class. Each student must come to the next class with around eight photocopies of their draft. With around 28 students in the class, we divide up into, say, eight small groups. This means that each group will then have one copy of each of the three or four compositions to be discussed that day.

In the first thirty minutes of these classes, students circulate the drafts in their small groups. They take notes, they discuss things, and someone from each group makes a list of key points raised by the group pertaining to each paper. For example, if we are working on drafts by "Dave," "Alicia," and "Lani," here's how it would work:

Alicia, Dave, and Lani arrive—nervously, proudly, sometimes irritably—with eight copies of their drafts. Each small group gets one copy of each of these compositions. As "Carl," "Erica," and "Armand" read these drafts and discuss them, Carl will keep track of the key points on Alicia's draft, Erica will write down the key points on Dave's draft, and Armand will record the group's discussion of Lani's draft. The other groups in the class have done exactly the same thing.

After thirty or forty minutes, each group now has three or four lists and we're ready to begin our larger discussion.

We go around the room, taking up one of the compositions at a time, hearing each group's key points. The draft's author doesn't say anything but is expected to take notes and jot down any questions he or she may wish to ask the class. Each composition gets about 10 or 12 minutes of this kind of hearing. At the end of class, the authors take home the lists of key points to refer to in revising their work. They are free to use as many or as few of the suggestions as they like, and they attach the suggestions to the end of their final drafts so I can see the kinds of choices they made. Again, for example, Lani will take home around eight sheets of notes on her draft, one from each group. She will revise, either for homework or during the next class (depending on the particular assignment and/or project), and in doing so, will have to make some choices about the changes she wishes to make. Whatever revisions she makes, she will attach the eight sheets of suggestions to her final draft. When I read through her composition, I may consult the suggestion sheets to see the kinds of critiques she received and how much, or little, Lani opted to take up these suggestions.

There may be three such workshop classes in a row before the class holds an intensive in-class writing and editing day.

Writing and editing days consist mainly of students working on drafts in class. They may be working on their own drafts, in which case they may work alone or with one partner. Students may also be working on their larger projects—pamphlets, books, and so on. In these cases, students may work in slightly larger groups, discussing revisions, edits, lay-outs, covers, or any feature of the project under hand. If I am specifically invited to sit in on a group, I do so. Otherwise, I may speak with individual students, write a few general suggestions on the board, or read a piece of writing a student has given me to look over.

What do students write in these pamphlets and books? Somewhat like yours, mine write about something "important" that they want their readers to know about from their (the students') perspective. One year, a group came up with an "advertisement" pamphlet: it was an elaborate fold-out "map" of a futuristic prison system that "guaranteed" rehabilitation of inmates. The twenty-five page text, accompanied by drawings, a photograph, and "testimonials" by former "inmates," was a carefully researched bit of writing which drew upon our Theme Lecture's class readings on the history of prisons in America and on the Theme Lecture trip to Eastern State Penitentiary in Philadelphia (which for many of my students is their first trip outside of New York City).

For these projects, I inevitably have to keep extra office hours because small, collaborating groups often want conferences with me to discuss their progress. But we also get a lot of this kind of consultation done right in the class. Toward the end of the semester, I can't tell you how many times a student will groan, saying, "You're killing me!" And yet, at the end of the term, when we share the books, celebrate, read parts out loud, and invite others in to hear, students are clearly, and rightfully, proud. And when I tell them that they have accomplished something remarkable and that they can now "live it up" a little, they know it's true, and they know that *I know* it's true, too.

Michael

———————————

Michael:

You know, I don't remember either of us ever writing to each other about how we run our composition classes. Strange, isn't it? I remember something you wrote about how you tell students that composing in writing is a lot like building a physical structure. I mean, composition theory interests me, but I have to say that it's refreshing to remember that composition classes, like structures, are held together by something; I'm glad we've traded these "nuts and bolts." Writing about my comp classes has actually been energizing. After all, I've been building this pedagogy for twenty years, and it feels like a relief to unpack it in this way.

Mark

———————————

Mark:

It's great to see the students puff up a bit at the end of the semester when they have completed their books, isn't it? Last year I held a book-signing party at the end of the semester. Since students make three copies of their final book projects for my class, I get to keep one. (Students keep one for themselves, unmarked. I write comments in another copy, and the third, unmarked copy, goes into my office library). So, at this book-signing party, I got everyone to sign my copy of their books. They really got a bit full of themselves at these parties, and I was happy enough to supply the occasion.

Michael

———————————

Mark:

It occurred to me, thinking about these books, that our students do not simply write what they are "burning to tell the world." For one thing, who, or what, *is* "the world" for them, for any of us? I would suggest that our students are, in effect, writing what they are burning to be told, in a way that finally makes some sense to them. They are, necessarily, projecting themselves out into "the world" so as to be the kind of reader or listener who can not only understand the message, but who will attend to it largely because of the way in

which the message is delivered. This is not a criticism, obviously. The useful-
ness, for me, in this idea is that it gives me an insight into the choices our
students make for how they put together their compositions. It provides me
with an agenda for reading these compositions as indicators for how our
students may be imagining "the world." It certainly provides food for thought
with regard to the ways in which our students conceive of potential readers
and listeners, conversants and correspondents. I imagine that our students'
compositions are not only about things they are burning to tell, but about their
ideas on how such things must be introduced into "the world's" conversations.

I am now thinking of the end of Creeley's poem, "Anger," where he writes:

> All you say you want
> to do to yourself you do
> to someone else as yourself
>
> and we sit between you
> waiting for whatever will
> be at last the real end of you. (309)

Michael

Michael:

Do you remember that early on this semester I wrote to tell you about a
student in my class who wanted to write her book about how her boyfriend
had beaten her up and how she was dealing with it? Well, Andrea has finished
her book.

Andrea's book contains harrowing descriptions of this man's abusive phone
calls to her, his stalking her when she broke off with him, and, finally, what
happened one night when he drove her car off the road.

> Jack approached my car everything was in slow motion. I turned to look
> at him and with a closed fist and all his might he punched my left
> temple. I was instantly woozey. Confused. Screaming in pain I block out
> what he was yelling. I couldn't move, I have my seat belt on, my legs
> under the steering wheel and Jack on top of me beating my face to a
> bloody mess. I managed to free my legs and I started to kick. Both of us
> covered in my blood. I got Jack off of me. I whipped my car into drive
> almost hitting Jack I drove through some guy's yard. I was approaching
> a hill when I noticed Jack was beside me. He tried to run me off the
> road. I swurved in to the oncoming lane and over the hill I went. He tried
> again to run me off the road into a cow pasture while trying to get away I
> hit a deer but it was the best thing that could have happened because it
> jammed both the driver side doors. Flying down the road I started to
> brake to turn into my drive way. Jack sped up and made sure I didn't get
> in because he was blocking it with his car. I drove my car across the
> street threw my neighbor's yard, making a U-turn into the driveway

beside mine. Almost taking out their white picket fence Jack was close behind. I was half way in the driveway when I couldn't go any more I was saturated with blood from my face. My eyes were swelling shut. I couldn't see any thing but Jack was trying to open the door. He was pounding and screaming at the top of his lungs and believe it or not he didn't wake even a single soul. After about ten minutes he got in the car and drove off. Scared as hell I climbed out of my car and ran to the neighbors house screaming hysterically and ring the door bell like a maniac, someone let me in. Dripping blood all over the floor I tried to call my mom, but she was in bed because it was after 1:15 in the morning. I called Adam while Mr. Spreng (my neighbor) went to wake my mom up. I got hold of Adam and explained what had happened, he called the police and the hospital. He was at my house moments later. I finally got into my house as my mom was coming down the stairs. I told her briefly what had happened, she got dressed and I was on my way to the hospital. I was cleaned up and taken to x-ray to find out that Jack broke my nose, fractured my jaw, and left me with bone chips and splinters around my eye sockets.

The book then goes on to cover the aftermath of this incident:

I went to the courthouse. I won the case. That was the first time I had seen Jack since he beat me up. I was filled with fright, I was so scared I was crying and shaking so bad. I couldn't stop. I went to the bathroom that made everything worse than before because I looked in the mirror. I was purple and swollen. I looked like the elephant man. I had no idea who I was, I felt robbed. "Was I ever going to look the same? Could I ever be the happy go lucky person that I was? What was I going to do?"

In her book, Andrea talks about her feelings of uncertainty at the trial, where she had to testify:

The first hearing I had to face Jack and tell my story. I stood up, took a deep breath "Oh my gosh. Why did this happen to me? What was I going to say?" I froze, I couldn't do it. Yes I could I have to, He deserves it. He had no right. The words just started to flow.

Jack is convicted.
Andrea's book ends this way:

. . . I'm in counseling, trying to get myself back together. I still have one more surgery to go the doctors now think that I should have my jaw rebroken and splinted. After all this time I still have never heard Jack's reasons for beating me up that's probally something I will never know either. Over time I have forgiven Jack but I will never have respect for him again. Love?
    Love is patient, love is kind. . .

Michael, today was quite a class for Andrea. It began with her coming to tell me that she missed the last class session because she was in court. Jack was sentenced. He will be in jail 3 months to a year, with five years of probation.

Something good happened later in the hour. I had put the class into peer response groups so that students could read each other's drafts and write suggestions for revision on them. (We are currently working on the second book for the class.) I was sitting in a group near Andrea's. Jennifer came over and asked if she could borrow Andrea's book—that she *really* wanted to read it. Andrea was sitting right near by. She looked up. I gave Jennifer the book and went over to her and asked how it made her feel that someone *really* wanted to read her book. She said, "Terrific."

Mark

PS I have been thinking about how you responded when you read these excerpts from Andrea's book. It is a bit rough, isn't it? I am particularly unnerved, or moved, as a reader, though, by the tense shifts. It is as if Andrea, even as she wrote and revised (and, yes, she might have done more of this, as I discussed with her), could not totally extricate herself from the past—as if she is still there, that night, even as she is, chronologically, in its wake and trying, as she says, to find herself again. As for the revision process, I know that it has been affected by the time and energy she has spent in the hospital and in therapy and in court this semester. Grading this book was very difficult. Andrea herself, as she wrote in her self-evaluation, felt that the book should be assigned a B. I, too, independently arrived at the same grade through my evaluation. (I don't know what grades my students assign their work until after I have reached a grade.) It was hard to assign a grade of B in this case because the subject matter is so personal. I also felt the grade should reflect the scope of the project and Andrea's attention to its overall design. Still, I recognize that the very nature of the writing my students choose to do complicates the grading process in sometimes uncomfortable ways.

Mark

Mark:

I'm trying to imagine what I would do in your situation, with regard to Andrea's book. Did you ever consider giving Andrea an extension? I have done this. I might say to the student something like, "OK, you have brought your project along this far. You've done the hardest work of all—you've written about something deeply personal and troubling. Now I would like to see you revise it so that it can more closely reflect the effort you've put in so far. You may find that the revision feels a lot more like what, and how, you wanted to present all along. Would you like some time to go and do it?" Sometimes, my students say yes and sometimes no, but I leave the decision to them.

Michael

Michael:

Good idea, Michael. As a matter of fact I offer extensions sometimes. This was one time, however, where I thought I had gotten all I could out of the student. I may have been wrong; the book needed work.

Here's another story about grading. A student of mine, Sharon, wrote her book, *The Death of a Dream,* on the death of her father. Sharon tells how she grew up not knowing her natural father, which was no immediate concern to her as a child because she loved her stepfather, a good man, very much. In fact her home life with him was wonderful.

As Sharon grew older, she began to wonder about her natural father and the potential half-siblings she might have in the world. When she turned eighteen, her mother gave Sharon permission to find her natural father. But getting permission and acting upon it were two different things. Sharon's life was a full one, and it took her a year to decide to finally commit to finding her father—in January. The problem is that Sharon's mother was contacted by her ex-husband's family and was told that Sharon's father was murdered in a motel in Virginia on Christmas Eve. Sharon writes:

> I thought a lot about this over the next few days. I began to feel guilty. If I had not procrastinated . . . if I had gotten over the fear of the truth instead of letting it rule my life—if I had made the first step to contact the family, maybe he would have been with family on Christmas Eve, and not in the Ramada Inn with a killer roommate. I began to convince myself it was all my fault. . . .

Sharon returned to IUP for the spring break in the middle of this confusion. In fact, she came back to school earlier than her roommate so that she was alone. Her first night back, she lay awake all night in her empty room, scared, confused, feeling guilty, and crying. The next morning she resumed her college life: "No one could tell that there was anything wrong during the day, but every night I would cry myself to sleep—quietly, so my roommate wouldn't know."

OK, so now you know a bit about this book. The architecture of the book is solid (chapters make sense, work together, etc.). The chronology is intricate but clear (well-timed digressions). The design is elegant (the book demonstrates care in every detail of its appearance: cover art, font choices, layout of dedication page). Here's the problem: how I evaluated and graded the book. The book really ends pretty weakly, with a pat conclusion in which Sharon says how much she has changed, without ever really saying how. It seemed to me that the writer ran out of time. In addition, there are a few editing issues to which Sharon might have attended. I decided to assign a B+. I then saw that Sharon herself assigned a B in her self-evaluation, saying what I had said to myself: weak conclusion, more editing. That might have been the end of it, but it wasn't. For the past month I have returned to the grade on several occasions. I have been thinking that something is wrong. Finally, two days ago I asked Sharon to come to my office to talk about her book some more. In this conversation she told me that she still thinks that the conclusion is weak, but she also said that she now thinks she knows why. You see, her father had only been dead about two months at the writing of her book. She said that she simply had no very solid conclusion to make, and that if I asked her to make one today, she still wouldn't be able to do so.

It made sense. Because this is school, I had expected Sharon to make sense of this profound experience in her life according to the time schedule of assignments and grades. But what does such an experience have to do with grade books? Sharon may never come to a conclusion on the subject of her father. Who could blame her? I surely was expecting a lot of understanding of life and death from this young student.

During the course of the conversation I found out some other things about this book and this student. Sharon had given a copy of her book to her mother, who cried as she read it. Sharon and her mother then sat at a computer together and went through and proofread and edited the book. Sharon's mother then took the book and had a hardbound copy made for Sharon. So the book became this object of work and love between mother and daughter.

I am changing the grade to A.

Mark

—————————————

Mark:

One of my students, Diana, entitled her book, *Someone to Watch Over Me: When a Teen's Life Isn't Worth Living*. It's a remarkable work for several reasons—the obvious one is that it's an eloquent account of inner suffering and doubt, of despair. But there's something more, which I'll tell you after I quote a bit from the book.

In her introduction, she writes:

> The summer before I turned 14, my demon entered my life. It threat-
> ened to squeeze my life from me. It kept me awake all night, never
> letting me forget its existence.

With that dramatic start to things, she continues further down the page:

> Nothing I do matters. I can't change anything.

And still further along, she writes:

> There are lots of books about how at 13 girls fall off a cliff and sink into
> some kind of adolescent abyss. We no longer do well in math, we hate
> our bodies, we fight with our parents and take up deviant behavior. We
> go from precious little angels to become male-hungry devils. The book
> lays blame on everything from hormones to television for our sudden
> feelings of doubt.

> All I am left to do was brace myself for whatever they throw my way.
> For me that is what it meant to be a black girl. . . . I am nobody and I
> don't get to be in charge of anything, and not being in charge of
> anything is the worst thing in the world.

Diana goes on to describe her experience of finding a book in a library entitled
Growing Up Dead: A Hard Look at Why Adolescents Commit Suicide. In that
book, she reads about one young man who kept a journal, and she comes to
regard that young man, Peter, as her "friend." When she reads more of the
book, more of Peter's journals, she becomes more convinced that he speaks
to her, for her. And when the book's author detailed Peter's subsequent
suicide, Diana writes:

> I'm devastated, but I imagine and admire his courage. There is the
> obvious nerve of taking a gun and pressing it to your temple. But I'm
> more fascinated by the courage to tell someone, anyone, that some-
> thing is wrong. That's what Peter did; pulled the trigger and said, I hurt
> this much. He obviously knew what he wanted to say. On the other
> hand, I have no idea how to say anything to anyone. I cannot speak the
> words from my mouth. I do not even know which words to use. All I
> know is something bad is happening to me.

The book continues, taking up Diana's loss of weight ("I am hungry but I
cannot eat. I tell my parents I'm not hungry. My Dad asks if I'm watching my
weight, I smile and tell him yes"). She finally attempts suicide:

> I swallow a thousand Advil pills. Actually it is only a hundred but I feel
> like I must die a thousand deaths. Dying is not really the point. I just
> don't know what else to do.

The attempt fails ("Even death cheats me"). She stops eating completely and
says that her body changes make her feel "powerful." Mark, her descent into
further pain is both fascinating and horrifying. She writes about contemplating
suicide again, razor blades, pills. Finally she thinks about "Peter," and she is
relieved to remember that she can use a gun.

And then, Mark, the shocker. She writes:

> I am not going to have to live like this anymore. I make a list of who is
> going to get what: my Cds, my books, my teddy bears, the money in my
> bank account. I tell them how I want to be buried. I want to sleep beside
> my grandmother.
>   The Wednesday before Christmas 1990 on the day of her 18th
> birthday, my best friend killed herself.

I had no idea what was going on, Mark. Was Diana writing this narrative in the
first person voice of her dead friend? Was she trying to imagine what her
friend had been experiencing? Was the "best friend" actually a facet of Diana
herself? She is such a fine writer, it would not have surprised me to learn she
had been writing about a metaphorical "self" she had killed so that another,
healthier one could live. In other words, I did not know what to think. Was the
entire book a notice—a warning—that this young woman needed help
immediately?

At JJC, we have a number of fine counselors. I called one and asked him what he recommended I do in response to this paper. He suggested I follow my instincts and call Diana. He said there was certainly nothing wrong with expressing my concern over content so dramatic and so tragic. He also suggested I encourage Diana to come in and talk to a counselor.

I called her. She seemed surprised, even a little alarmed, that I was calling. She is a very shy, quiet, and incredibly bright young woman, a Jamaican who has written about growing up as a girl in a country that "treats men and boys like kings and princes and treats girls like future sex-partners, baby-makers, and broken hearts." I told her I'd had a chance to read through her book and that it was beautifully written but also deeply troubling. She asked, "You thought it was disturbing?"

It was hard to read her voice, Mark. I guess I'd expected that either she'd be relieved to be able to talk openly about the book or she'd be completely reluctant to discuss it. Instead, she seemed almost intrigued that her words had had this effect on someone. I asked her whether the book had been about her friend, as it seemed, or if it was more metaphorical. She said, "It's about my friend." I asked her about her decision to write the first 90% of it in the first person, without quotation marks, before suddenly switching to third person. She said, "Was that a bad thing to do?"

Of course I told her that it was *not* a bad thing to do, that it was a profoundly effective way to convey the immediacy of the experience, that I had been thinking all along that I was reading about Diana, herself, and was actually disoriented when the narrative switched at the end. I asked her about the introductory sections which seemed to echo other things Diana has written about her childhood. She said, "Well, I guess some of the book is about me. Some of it is kind of a mixture."

Now I was worried again. But at least we were talking about it; she was interested in this conversation. We talked for around 15 minutes, about the book, about suicide, about the books on suicide Diana had read. At one point, I asked her if she'd ever spoken to a counselor about her loss after her friend's suicide. She seemed surprised by this. Evidently it had never occurred to her. And why should it have? Most of my students have little or no access to counseling other than the New York City Department Of Social Services, social workers and case workers who deal with foster care, child-abuse, domestic violence, the law. I told her that JJC has some excellent counselors, that the "fee" was already built into her student fees, and that she deserved to be able to talk things through just like anyone else who's been through a traumatic experience. She said, "Yeah, but this was six years ago. I should have gotten counseling back then, right?" I told her that her book suggested that her grief was still acute, and that she has so many insightful things to say about her own feelings, she would probably derive a great deal of comfort from counseling at this point. To my surprise, she agreed.

This semester, Diana is in three of my classes. When I mentioned to her that it's a good idea to "diversify" a little when it comes to undergraduate courses and teachers, she said, "Don't worry, I'm not going to be a groupie. I just really like the topics of your courses." I have to smile, now, when I think about that, because it was, by far, the most confident thing Diana has ever said to me! She is doing really well in all her classes, and I'm beginning to think her book really had been written as a way to express her confusion and grief over her friend's suicide. From things Diana has written about subsequently, I gather that her own childhood involved some similarities to her friend's.

Michael

Michael:

I was as interested in reading the story of your trying to figure out how to read, and then what to do about, Diana's riveting narrative as I was in her narrative itself. Not to minimize for one second Diana's story, but I think the one you tell about feeling disoriented by a student's writing is an important one. Look, sometimes there is no sure way to know whether such a piece of writing is: 1) a cry for help; 2) a call for attention; 3) intended to shock or entertain (I know, it's a morbid view of entertainment, but it's certainly a view shared by Hollywood and TV); or even, 4) an elaborate hoax. The only way I know to get at least a little closer to the truth is to do what you did, to investigate as thoroughly and as sensitively as possible.

I have this student, Bryan, who, also has written in his book about suicide, but Bryan is clearly writing about himself (seven years after his father, grandfather, and uncle have all died within three years of each other). He is not the writer that Diana is, but there is a directness in his work that has me on edge, especially where he describes how he has been affected by these deaths:

> Another change is I can no longer shed any tears. The last time I cried was at my father's burial. I did not even cry at my grandfather's or my uncle's funeral, and that makes me feel ashamed. I feel ashamed because everyone else was crying but I just stood there doing nothing.
> I let my problems build up and release it in a rage when I am pushed too far. I have not hit anyone but I have punched a lot of holes into walls and have had many verbal arguments with my mom and brother. The reason I let things build up is because I feel like I can't talk to anyone about it. It does not feel right to talk to my mom or brother about it because they might not understand my problems. They wouldn't understand because I have always felt like an outcast in the family. I still don't think that I fit in. I don't know if I could trust someone to truly open up to them. I won't open up to anyone because I might lose control over my emotions. I would rather keep them locked up and never open them again because I never resolved my emotions. I just buried them deep down inside me.
> When I am depressed, I like to get in my car and just drive to help clear my head because I am completely alone. One time I drove clear to

Virginia [from central Pennsylvania, Michael!]. Listening to music also helps to cheer me up because I can relate to some of the sad songs that I listen to.

Bryan is a quiet guy. When asked a question in class by me or one of the other students, he usually is silent for a minute, blushes and says, "I'm not sure" or "I don't know." If he offers an answer or response to a piece of writing, it is said in about as few words as possible. His first book was supposed to be twenty pages long; it turned out to be seven.

I had Bryan in my office to talk once. We talked about his book; then I told him about the counseling center. I asked him if he wanted to go, especially as he had written about suicidal thoughts and because he had been through a lot and could probably use someone to talk to, someone who would help him understand and deal with his loss. But he said no. The odd thing is that Bryan has dropped by on other occasions as well. Each time he sort of sits there, quietly smiling at me. I guess I sense he is after something more significant than small talk, so I always turn the talk back to the counseling center.

He says, "Maybe, I'll go, but probably not."
I ask him why.
He says, "Because I'm stubborn."
I ask him what that has to do with going or not going. He shrugs and smiles.

Yesterday he came at the end of the day as I was packing to leave school. I sat down. He seemed to have nothing or something to say—I couldn't tell which. He sat, asked me a question about a class assignment, and then, again, just sort of sat there.

After what felt like a period of uncomfortable silence, I asked him if he had been to the counseling center.
He said, "No" and smiled.
I smiled back and said, "Well, let's go together right now."
"No, I can't. I've got to go meet someone for dinner."
"Well, let's go after class on Thursday."
"No, I can't. I will be meeting someone for lunch." Smile.
"Well, let me know when and if you want me to go with you."
"OK." Smile.

There's nothing malicious in this smile. It's as if he enjoys—I don't know; I'm grasping for an understanding—this connection with me? this attention from a professor (I can imagine him trying to get as little attention as possible in his classes)? what? WHAT? Or better: WHY?

Clearly, I've got to go to the counseling center to get some help here.

His classmates have been terrific. Two different students read Bryan's book and both are responding respectfully and carefully to it. One is writing about how suicide is a waste (or something to that effect—I'll know more when I see the final version), and the other is writing about how it is not necessary for anyone to go without talking to someone—that there are friends and a counseling center on campus.

I don't know. I'm not so sure how things are going to turn out for Bryan—but then who can say? Here's the ending of his book:

> Well, these are my stories of lost loved ones. The weight of these deaths is a giant burden that will never go away. This weight feels like the whole world is about to come crashing down right on top of you and you can't control it. I hope they will help anyone going through this experience or that has gone through this process. Well I have said farewell to the ghosts of my past. As I said, it has been just past seven years since the death of my dad. I can't say if I did him proud over the last seven years because I really never accomplished much during this time. The only real accomplishment was graduating high school. I have changed a lot since my dad's death; some good some bad. I hope you have understood what I have gone through. It may help you to understand why I keep to myself.

I can't help but remember what Bryan wrote in his book about an occasion when he considered suicide but did not do it: ". . . sometimes I wish I had done it because my life sucks."

Mark

———————————

Michael:

A nervous Sunday morning. I am drinking coffee, sitting at the computer, looking out my window at my neighbors' roofs and thinking about a place I may have got things very wrong. Bryan finally agreed to go, but only after we had taken a casual walk across campus in the direction of the counseling center. I said something like, "Hey, here's the Counseling Center. Why don't we stop in and make an appointment?" I expected an elaborate refusal. He said, "Okay."

I am not saying that we are wrong in how we read our students' writing. I am not saying that our students are not in very real ways victimized, some of them every single day. And I am not saying that some of our students are not in real danger of committing suicide. And I am not saying that there are not times to intervene or do something—I am saying that there are also times in which we should do nothing (at least I think I am saying that). And this decision is complicated by the lack of time our students have and the lack of time we have in the midst of the classes we teach and the meetings we have. In all of this, I guess I want to say that my interactions with Bryan may indeed be a lesson in how oppressive care can be. I fear I may have forced him into signing up for care he didn't need. He may have signed up out of respect or as some kind of teacher-pleasing activity. The fact is that my students know things—whether they articulately word them or not. I've got to be a better listener.

Mark

Mark:

Sometimes we just have to tell our students that "it won't always be like this," that what they are experiencing is an angst that is part of living. I know that often we have to decide what to do for one student or another, and that the situation is high tension, and we feel as though we'd better get it right. Still, sometimes we have to trust ourselves to recognize a kind of teen angst that our students will simply have to go through.

Michael

Mark:

This is from Theresa's English 101 book, entitled *The Untold Secrets*. As you will see, the grammar is shaky, but this is a young woman who has been through "it." She came to my 101 class having taken 3 semesters to work her way through "remedial" English classes. I'm not sure how she passed them, but there she was. Her attendance wasn't great; her class participation was almost nothing unless someone addressed her specifically. On those occasions, she generally said, "I don't know" or just shrugged. Once in a while, she'd say something substantial; I would try to be as affirmative as possible on those occasions so that she would feel a little more inclined to contribute to the discussions and workshop sessions. It didn't help.

Here are excerpts from Theresa's book:

> Have you ever stopped to think and wonder what goes on in the lives of the many people you come across everyday of your life. You wonder what's going through their lives at that exact moment. You also wonder if their life was as much mess up as yours. Well I'am going to tell you a story about a young child who went from adolescent to adulthood in a short period of time while growing up. Furthermore, if you knew her or seen her she always seem happy. However, let me tell you, she was not. Maybe when you finish reading her story you would stop and wonder that people who seem happy in their lives are not always what it seems to be. . .

> The Mistake

> It's typical, my mother and father fell in love. She was 14 years of age and he was 21. However, they fell in love for all the wrong reasons. I

guess that's what happens when you are blinded by love. Furthermore, they stay together for many years and my brother was conceive. Everyone loved and adored him. He was the first born what did you expect. Then a year later, it came, the mistake, I was born. . . .

I was born premature. Three pounds and no ounces, now doesn't it seem to you that a mother who drank and smoke through out her pregnancy didn't care about her unborn child . . .

I gain my weight and after a month in the hospital they finally took me home. They should have just left me there or abandoned me or gave me up for adoption because as soon as I left the hospital that's when the nightmare of my fucking life began.

The Drugs

It all started when I was five, that's when I was aware of the things going on around me. The drugs, yes my father and no not my mother, they said she gave it up after I was born. . . . My father was . . . on crack cocaine. Not only was he using drugs, he was also selling them as well. Can you guess where? Well, he was selling them inside the apartment in which we lived. So, at the age of five, I have witness the strange people coming in and out of the apartment to buy the drugs. Not only did I witness them buying the drugs but I also witness them using them as well along with my father.

. . . Where was my mother? Do you know what her answer was when I ask her, she said she was working at the time. But knowing the situation and danger that I was in I ask her why didn't she just take me to a relative or even a friend's house knowing that I would be in good hands. Do you know what her damn response was, she had no one to take care of me. BULLSHIT! Is what I told her. She also said she had no control over my father and his drugs . . .

My father would rob and sell whatever we had just to get high and not only that he also took the rent money to pay the people he was selling from which he didn't pay back and so he almost got himself killed and us as well.

. . . One day I came home from school, yes by myself [six years old], what did you expect, I had no supervision. I came home and guess who I find drug up on the sofa, my father with a needle stuck in his arm. He had overdose from the crack that he had taken and I thought he was dead. I screamed and yelled, I knock on neighbors doors and they called the ambulance and they revive my father. He lived. It's weird because I loved my father but in a way I wish him dead because maybe it will all stop.

Do you think my father learned his lesson? No, I witness three more overdoses, one after the other and each time I wish him dead. Each time I wish him dead.

The Abuse

When I was seven . . . I started seeing the abuse. You think the drugs were bad, no I don't think so! Now there was the alcohol that turn my father into the violent man he became.

He started abusing my mother for the slightest thing. Why wasn't the food done on time? Why weren't we sleeping?

One night my father came home drunk and high on drugs and demanded my mother give him money to go get high. She refuse and so he punch her in the chest so hard she past out.

The Affair/Alone

I was about eight when my mother met him. That's when . . . I was left alone again. I guess she got tired of the abuse and so she went to seek love once again. Personally, I didn't approve at all. Why? Because despite what my father did and has done, I still loved my father and I expected the same from her at the time. So my mother left me alone with my brother in that apartment with a friend. You are probably saying to yourself, oh! She got smart, no I don't think so. I was still unsupervised because [the friend] was a drug user herself. Can you believe this? Not only did I have to cook, clean, take care of my brother who was older than I and my father as well. On top of that the lady that was supposedly watching me and my brother—I was watching her. I was only eight years old and this shit went on for two years.

Rebelling

I was about 13 going on 14. . . . I started to runaway. I also started experimenting on drugs and alochol because all my older friends were doing it.

Then I started meeting boys of all ages. That's when I met the biggest drug dealer on the block. Guess what I fell in love. I had everything, clothes, jewelry, money, and most of all I had something that no one really show me, LOVE. My mother found out and did not approve but she had no control over me.

I became pregnant at the age of 14. I didn't even know until I was 3 months. I was scared. My mother found out through people on the streets and she was upset. She told me I didn't exist and to tell my boyfriend to take care of it. Now you tell me was I loved and cared for? You figure it out. I wanted to keep my child and give it everything so I was undecided of what to do . . . I wanted to . . . finish school but I said to myself how would I do that if I have this child. So . . . on my 15th birthday, instead of celebrating the next day I was having an abortion. What a life for a 15 year old! I will never forget that day, I was scared, confused and angry all at the same time.

And it got worse because my mother decided to get my boyfriend arrested for statutory rape because I was 14 and he was 18 at the time.

> [Two years later], we decided to move . . . and I never saw him again,
> and so I was heartbroken. However, I found out later on that he had
> many other girls and gotten them pregnant as well. The bastard! I
> thought my world had ended and that's when I became suicidal. One
> night when everyone was asleep I went into the bathroom and took a
> whole bottle of sleeping pills. My brother find me and call 911 and I was
> rush to the hospital to have everything pump out of me.

Mark, Theresa ends her book by talking about her "recovery." As so many
students seem to believe, Theresa is convinced that her coming to college
means the end of the old life and the assurance of a new life. I recall Jim
Berlin talking about how much sleep he would lose over this misconception on
the part of his students. College assures very little, and certainly Theresa is
not headed for the "good life." In a way, she has had a slice of the "good life"
as Americans desire it: money, jewelry, someone to take care of her. Of
course, she had these things at age 14 and at the hands of a drug dealer, and
of course these things were possible only by way of the suffering of other
young people who were buying and using the crack her boyfriend was selling.
Still, Theresa believed college was the opening of a door she had only to walk
through to be in another life entirely. I have tried to find out if Theresa is still in
school. She's registered but has evidently not attended any classes this
spring.

You may be wondering about what I was thinking or doing throughout the
semester in which Theresa wrote this book. The thing is, she had turned in
very little work. I'd spoken to her many times, offered to refer her to a counselor, offered to help her with academic advisement. I listened to her reasons for
being absent or not having her assignments (the reasons were generally
vague—"trouble at home"—but I had a feeling that there was terrible stuff
happening to and with her). In other words, here was a student I could not
reach, who said "no thank you" to every offer of help or referral. And when I
asked to see her about her possibilities for passing English 101, she listened
quietly when I told her that there was almost nothing for me to offer in the way
of hope. By mid semester, she'd been absent four times and had turned in
one bit of writing to the workshop. She had kept a minimal journal, but opted
not to drop the course when I pointed out that she simply could not expect to
pass. I did not want to give her any false hopes.

I contacted the director of the Thematic Studies program, who is also our
program's social worker, who called Theresa at home to set up an appointment just to talk. Theresa didn't show to her appointment. One of our counselors offered to call and/or write to Theresa, suggesting an advisement meeting, presumably to deal with academic issues, but Theresa didn't show for that
appointment, either.

So, by the time we were three weeks from the end of the term, I'd seen maybe
5 pages of her writing. Her book proposal had been about "Teens and
Abortions"—a proposal so bland, I had trouble working with her on it. Her
peers sort of abandoned her; she was not providing even the minimum for
workshop discussions, and I have to admit I didn't think I could do anything for
her.

Her book was a surprise in that it obviously came from a decision she must have made to go for broke—to tell something "important" to her readers and to finish the course having at least said something substantial.

She and I talked over her options for a grade. She had not passed the course, as you can guess. By the end of the term, she'd been absent 7 times and had handed in less than half of the required minimum of material. The only thing I could think of was to give her an incomplete and let her retake the course as an audit, withholding her change of grade until well into the subsequent semester. I told her I had doubts about that course of action, but was willing to try if she was. She said she would rather just take the F and not have to worry about finishing an incomplete. She said she wasn't sure she was going to come back to school, that maybe she'd get a job and just work for a while, that she'd failed all but one of her other classes. My heart broke for this woman, Mark. I honestly felt I had no options for her. Again I asked her if she would like to talk with one of the counselors; again she said no thanks.

I'm not so self-centered to see Theresa's case as my failure, but I would be lying if I pretended not to feel despair where she is concerned. I don't know what else I could have done. Lots of people offered me advice. I took a good deal of the advice, but Theresa chose her own way.

As for those who might say they don't have time to teach to change the world, or to teach for peace, I can understand. Theresa was one of 104 students I had that semester—29 in English 101, 33 in my Lit course, 27 in my Theme Lecture group, and 15 in my Internship practicum. She was not the only student whose prospects were slim-to-none. She was not the worst writer. But her case touches me where I live. And although I honestly did not have the time it would have taken to work more successfully with Theresa, I had to try, as I have to try every time, with each student. That sounds pretty pathetic but where is the "happy medium"? Where do we draw the line?

Michael

Michael:

The story you tell of Theresa, the book she has written, it all just hammers home the idea that some of our students, despite their talents, despite their and our best efforts and those of our colleagues, despite everything, are just lost to us. I know you do not easily accept her giving up on school, and I wouldn't either. Perhaps, sadly, she decided that school offers little to somebody who survives ordeals such as hers.

Mark

PS Thought you might like to know: Bryan stayed after his exam today and told me that he has started the counseling, that it is tough, and that he is going to keep going.

At one point in his book *Amazing Grace: The Lives of Children and the Conscience of a Nation,* Jonathan Kozol talks to Anthony, a precocious 12-year-old Latino boy, about life in the Bronx. Anthony says:

> "Sadness is one plague today. Desperate would be a plague. Drugs are a plague also, but the one who gets it does not have to be the firstborn. It can be the second son. It could be the youngest."
>
> "Anthony, what should we do to end this plague?"
>
> "Mr. Jonathan," he answers, "only God can do that. I cannot be God." I ask him when he thinks this plague will end "or else go some place else."
>
> "Mr. Jonathan," he says again, "I don't know when. I think it will only happen in the Kingdom of Heaven, but even the angels do not know when that will come. I only know that this is not His kingdom."
>
> "How can you be sure of that?" I ask.
>
> "This," he says with a gesture out the window that seems to take in many things beyond the dealers on the sidewalk and the tawdry-looking storefront medical office just across the street, "this out here is not God's kingdom. A kingdom is a place of glory. This is a place of pain." (84)

And what about the expressions of this pain? We see some of it in writings, yes. But we *don't* see so much of it—certainly not in direct proportion to the pain experienced by some of the students we've met over the years. Michael's student, Theresa, did not have the ability to pass English 101 that semester. Michael advised her that she had little chance in the course, that she really ought to be spending lots of time in the writing center, that her other courses were going to be affected, and so on. She agreed, she knew, she accepted, she stayed.

At the end of the semester, in her book, she wrote for nearly twenty pages about the "hidden life" people can have—and about her own life— her home. A place of pain.

Mark:

I had seen very little of Theresa's outlines, notes, etc., and should not have accepted the book because she followed zero of the procedures we'd all agreed to, but I did accept it. When all the books were on display in the front of the room at our end-of-term book party, I said, "I'm a little surprised to see your book, Theresa." I had meant that I didn't know she had intended to complete it. But she thought that I'd somehow (miraculously) read through it even though it had just shown up that afternoon. She said, "Yeah, you could say pain wrote most of it."

Michael

Maybe some of the kinds of pain our students go through are kinds that cannot find a public register. We find that for some students we may have solutions, but for others we may not even perceive the problem. This realization chills us. David B. Morris writes, "What surprised me most when I began my research at the pain clinic of a large university hospital was the apparently normal faces of the patients" (67). He continues, "It is not a pleasant trait, but we sometimes feel suspicious of people who say they are in pain but who do not groan or writhe or pound the floor" (68).

We are under no illusion that our composition classes are "pain clinics"; we are neither physicians nor counselors. We are teachers of writing who are in the mire of living complicated lives and learning a difficult craft. We are teachers of writing and writers who write to work our own way through the difficult times. This is what we can share with our students. But there can be no pretending that pain is not at the center of too many of our students' lives. Some might say that we pay far too much attention to the lives of our students and not enough attention to teaching them skills; we permit too much emoting, and we don't teach students to hone their professional, impersonal voices in exposition. Others might say we are reading "pain" into texts, or that we are, in fact, encouraging our students to frame their experiences in pain-filled ways. Still others might echo Ann Murphy's caution that the work composition teachers do can sometimes be "a profoundly personal intrusion, one which combines the powers of psychology, state, and education to impinge on their innermost selves" (187). We certainly understand these concerns. We don't necessarily disagree. We can only say, in response, that if *you* were asked to write something "important," something you are "burning to tell the world," and if what you wrote was a narrative of suffering, surely you would not want us to call it something else. If you were to write about having suffered terrible abuse, about having been neglected, addicted, incarcerated, lonely, suicidal, lost, surely you would not want us to overlook the life that put fingers to keyboard in telling that story any more than you should wish us to overlook the life behind the telling of triumph, of safety, of joy, of success. For us, writing is always also living, and as teachers who prize the writing our students do, we can't help but prize the lives of the writers. This is what we are burning to tell you: that we must teach for the living.

Michael:

Sometimes—I am tempted to say many times—I have had first year students come to me quietly and separately in class when they are responding to the personal writing of a colleague and say, "I don't know how to respond to this piece of writing." It is always such a curious moment. I ask them why, and they usually say something like, "It's so personal." To which I usually say, "Is that a bad thing?" They say, "No." Then I say, "Why not tell the writer how their writing makes you feel?"

OK—I need to try to work something out here. Sometimes my students don't know how to respond to writing that asks them to feel. It is not enough, I have found—perhaps too slowly in my teaching career—to teach students how to respond to the technical aspects of any piece of writing. I must also teach some students how important it is to respond to writing that asks them to feel. To put this another way, I have to teach them how to "be there." By being there, I am not thinking of popular psychology as much as the phenomeno-logical problem of being present for writers. It means, sometimes, writing a personal letter to the writer at the end of the piece the student is reading. Sharing something personal of your own in response. Giving something back.

I have seen amazing examples of the kind of being there I am talking about—one of the most astounding was in a composition class where a student handed out a paper for a whole class workshop. That paper contained a couple of sentences which capture the feel of the whole. The author wrote that when she looks in the mirror, she doesn't see what others see. She sees someone hideous. The paper was filled with torturous statements of the student's self-loathing. The day of the workshop, the class, in its circle, tried valiantly to do its work. One by one, they praised the paper for its honesty and offered suggestions for revision. As the class was ending, one of the women in the class went over to the writer and silently put her arms around her. She was followed by another, then another, until there were, I am not sure how many, four? six? women standing in the middle of the room, the writer in the middle of these women all with their arms around each other.

Mark

Mark:

In Kozol's book, he talks frequently with Mrs. Washington. She is quite unhealthy, suffers from AIDS, but is struggling to raise her child (who is, tragically, also struggling to keep his mother alive). At one point, Kozol and Mrs. Washington are walking toward the subway after she has hurried him out of a bodega before a shooting begins (she noticed the robbery as it began to happen, and didn't want them to get caught in the crossfire). The conversation about life and death and conditions in the community is so important to her, she purchases a subway token just to keep walking Kozol to the platform so the discussion can continue. He then gets on the train, and she waves to him from the platform. That dollar and a half token was blood money for her. Perhaps he reimbursed her and simply did not mention it, but still, the gesture is telling (116–117).

The need to *testify* is so powerful, Mark. In her essay, "Organic Teaching," Sylvia Ashton-Warner reminds us, "It's just as easy for a teacher, who gives a child a brush and lets him paint, to give him a pencil and let him write, and to let him pass his story to the next one to read" (179). It's not just our students, of course. It's our need, too. It's the need of people everywhere in a culture that seems to have gone awry. Mrs. Washington spent food money (she was no longer using drugs and was really trying to bring some meaning to her life even as it was draining out of her) to carry on five minutes more of talk with a writer who would, in whatever way he'd promised, carry her stories into the wide world.

Michael

Michael:

I think you are on to something here. In fact, your offering of this term, "testifying," makes something a bit clearer to me about my own teaching. Most of my students really do come, though at various points in the process, to value their books, not just as objects (even art objects) that they have made, though that is a feeling worth paying attention to in and of itself, but also as evidence (testimony) to the significance of their lives. For many of them, the books are a way to record the meaning, literally, of their presence on Earth. The books are places to evidence either the pains they have endured or some good that they have done or seen—and then to interpret these experiences— to assign significance.

Let me give you an example of a book that does both: bears witness to pain and tells of love and family. In *Trying Times: A Struggle for Strength,* Rochelle writes about living with her grandmother—and then the memory:

> In October of my senior year, my cousin got shot in the head and in the back right down the street from my grandma's house. It seemed to be an attempted robbery, but the police didn't know. I was upset with what was going on and I cried all the time. My grandma was the worst with the news. She didn't really comment about what happened, but I knew she was very upset because that was her grandchild.
> At the funeral, I was the only one to see my grandma come and leave. She came before everyone to view his body because she was very ill. That day, she didn't even go to the burial where he was buried over the top of my cousin who got killed in front of my grandma's door by his friend and some girl two years before this. This was too much of a tragedy for my grandma to have two grandkids killed by violence near home where they came to have fun and see her.

I think that this need to testify runs to the very heart of the living. And Michael, for my white, rural, western Pennsylvanian students, reading and talking about an African American classmate's experiences related on such a personal, heartfelt level was, quite obviously, unsettling. These were not abstractions about urban life from the TV news; these were the words and the life of a classmate, someone they had come to care about.

Mark

In her essay, "Cultural Narratives Passed On: African American Mourning Stories," Karla Holloway writes:

> Our communities offer up these tragically wounded spirits every day as our children fall victim to a national culture of violence. The familiar shapes are their bodies. The recognizable spaces are our neighborhoods and homes. We shudder knowing the brutal familiarity of gunshots, and we have learned to tremble hearing the echo of sirens. All of us have learned to share in the language of mourning—witness the processions in our churches and the gatherings around caskets. The familiar literary theme of a character's quest for identity is revised in the African American narrative to a body's search for a safe harbor. There is not only psychic drama here, but physical necessity. (37)

Holloway addresses the importance of—and the sorrow inherent in—the many mourning stories laced through African American literature. Specifically, she notes the powerful role that the bodies of the deceased play in the cultural narrative of African American experience. Mourning stories, whether in literature or in the daily telling of our African American students, friends, lovers, and neighbors, form what Holloway calls "the character of our cultural bodies" (38). And as we have argued here and elsewhere, it is up to all of us who place ourselves in the position to read and try to comprehend these stories to be ready not to understand but also not to remove ourselves to the safety of a merely editorial stance. We are going to have to face up to the task of poring over evidence upon evidence of violence and sorrow, to the "social and aesthetic construction of mourning" (39) played out again and again, even in the writings of young students. As Holloway reminds us, "Only a culture that could be even arguably identified with violence and abuse would find its aesthetic expression . . . ironically and perversely sustained through telling these stories of death and dying" (38).

But can we continue to read stories of pain for years into the future without becoming callused or burned out? Yet how would we shut them off? If we tell our students not to write these stories for us to read, what will we have them write that will be worth reading? And what would we have them *read* that would be worth reading? You can't get away from the pain. But you can't ignore that all of these students in all that they write are living, and they believe that they will be read, and that what they say matters.

We have children. We know what kinds of violence can be in their lives—we have to remain vigilant each and every day to be sure they aren't victimized as some of our students have been. It is scary to say this, but we don't want our children to live as our students have lived. Our students don't want others to live as they have lived.

Our students are warning us. They are not pretending when they tell us and each other, again and again—in their books, their conversations, their faces—that their daily matters are life and death. We cannot afford to lose these stories; to do so is to lose our students' histories, to lose our own bearings in the present, to lose the material that might give us hope for the future. Our students' compositions are the most poignant kind of letters for the living. What they need to know is that there is still someone living out there to respond. That someone *will* respond. That *we* will respond. That *you* will.

Note

1. We recognize that assigning book making projects is not unique to us; in fact, our teaching is influenced by the countless creative elementary, middle school, high school, and college teachers we have met over the years who also involve students in bookmaking projects.

Works Cited

Abbott, Philip. *Seeking Many Inventions: The Idea of Community in America*. Knoxville: University of Tennessee Press, 1987.

Allende, Isabel. "Writing as an Act of Hope." *Rethinking Peace*. Eds. Robert Elias and Jennifer Turpin. Boulder and London: Lynne Rienner Publishers, 1994. 184–93.

Asante, Molefi Kete. *The Afrocentric Idea*. Philadelphia: Temple University Press, 1987.

Ashton-Warner, Sylvia. "Organic Teaching." *Radical School Reform*. Eds. Ronald and Beatrice Gross. New York: Simon & Schuster, 1969. 178–89.

Attali, Jacques. *Millennium: Winners and Losers in the Coming World Order*. Trans. Leila Conners and Nathan Gardels. New York: Times Books, 1991.

Berlin, James A. "Composition Studies and Cultural Studies: Collapsing Boundaries." *Into the Field: Sites of Composition Studies*. Ed. Anne Ruggles Gere. New York: Modern Language Association, 1993. 99–116.

———. "Contemporary Composition: The Major Pedagogical Theories." *College English* 44.8 (1982): 765–77.

———. *Rhetoric and Reality: Writing Instruction in American Colleges, 1900–1985*. Carbondale, IL: Southern Illinois University Press, 1987.

———. "Rhetoric, Poetic, and Culture: Contested Boundaries in English Studies." *The Politics of Writing Instruction: Postsecondary*. Eds. Richard H. Bullock and John Trimbur. Portsmouth, NH: Boynton/Cook, 1991. 23–38.

———. *Rhetorics, Poetics, and Cultures: Refiguring College English Studies*. Urbana, IL: National Council of Teachers of English, 1996.

———. Transcript. In Hurlbert and Blitz. *Composition and Resistance*. 137.

———. *Writing Instruction in Nineteenth–Century American Colleges*. Studies in Writing and Rhetoric. Carbondale, IL: Southern Illinois University Press, 1984.

Bishop, Wendy. *Released into Language: Options for Teaching Creative Writing*. Urbana, IL: National Council of Teachers of English, 1990.

Blitz, Michael, and C. Mark Hurlbert. "To Make a Home: The Role of Listening in Cultural Studies." *Cultural Studies and Composition: Conversations in Honor of James Berlin*. Special issue of *Works and Days 27/28* 14.1 & 2 (1996): 269–79.

Brock-Utne, Birgit. *Educating for Peace: A Feminist Perspective*. New York: Pergamon Press, 1985.

Buber, Martin. "Dialogue." *Between Man and Man*. New York: Collier, 1965. 1–39.

Byrd, Don. "Manifesto: Culture War." Unpublished manuscript. 1992.

———. *The Poetics of the Common Knowledge*. Albany, NY: State University of New York Press, 1994.

Cain, Mary Ann. *Revisioning Writers' Talk: Gender and Culture in Acts of Composing*. Albany, NY: State University of New York Press, 1995.

Castoriadis, Cornelius. *Crossroads in the Labyrinth*. Trans. Kate Soper and Martin H. Ryle. Cambridge, MA: MIT Press, 1984.

Coetzee, J. M. *In the Heart of the Country*. New York: Penguin, 1977.

Creeley, Robert. "Anger." *The Collected Poems of Robert Creeley: 1945–1975*. Berkeley: University of California Press, 1982. 305–9.

Delpit, Lisa D. *Other People's Children: Cultural Conflict in the Classroom*. New York: New Press, 1995.

Derkson, Daniel John, and Victor C. Strasburger. "Media and Television Violence: Effects on Violence, Aggression, and Antisocial Behaviors in Children." In Hoffman. 61–78.

Downing, David B., ed. *Changing Classroom Practices: Resources for Literary and Cultural Studies*. Refiguring English Studies. Ed. Stephen M. North. Urbana, IL: National Council of Teachers of English, 1994.

Downing, David B., and James J. Sosnoski, with Keith Dorwick, eds. *Cultural Studies and Composition: Conversations in Honor of James Berlin*. Spec. issue of *Works and Days 27/28* 14.1&2 (1996).

Epp, Juanita Ross, and Ailsa M. Watkinson, eds. *Systemic Violence in Education: Promise Broken*. SUNY Series, Education and Culture: Critical Factors in the Formation of Character and Community in American Life. Eds. Eugene F. Provenzo, Jr., and Paul Farber. Albany, NY: State University of New York Press, 1997.

Faigley, Lester. "Competing Theories of Process: A Critique and a Proposal." *College English* 48.6 (1986): 527–42.

——. *Fragments of Rationality: Postmodernity and the Subject of Composition*. Pittsburgh Series in Composition, Literacy, and Culture. Pittsburgh: University of Pittsburgh Press, 1992.

Felson, Richard B., and James T. Tedeschi. "A Social Interactionist Approach to Violence: Cross Cultural Applications." In Ruback and Weiner. 153–70.

Friday, Jennifer C. "Weapon-Carrying in Schools." In Hoffman. 21–32.

Frym, Gloria. "Training for the Apocalypse." *Up Late: American Poetry Since 1970*. 2nd ed. Ed. Andrei Codrescu. New York: Four Walls Eight Windows, 1989. 221.

Fu, Danling. *"My Trouble Is My English": Asian Students and the American Dream*. Portsmouth, NH: Boynton/Cook, 1995.

Futrell, Mary Hatwood. "Violence in the Classroom: A Teacher's Perspective." In Hoffman. 3–20.

Gessner, David. "A June Journal." *Creative Nonfiction 7: Points of View* (1996): 49–61.

Gradin, Sherrie L. *Romancing Rhetorics: Social Expressivist Perspectives on the Teaching of Writing*. Portsmouth, NH: Boynton/Cook, 1995.

Hawkes, Terence. *Structuralism and Semiotics*. Berkeley: University of California Press, 1977.

Hoffman, Allan M., ed. *Schools, Violence, and Society*. Westport, CT: Praeger, 1996.

Hollingsworth, Sandra. *Teacher Research and Urban Literacy Education: Lessons and Conversations in a Feminist Key*. New York: Teachers College Press, 1994.

Holloway, Karla F. C. "Cultural Narratives Passed On: African American Mourning Stories." *College English* 59.1 (1997): 32–40.

hooks, bell. "An Interview with bell hooks by Gloria Watkins: No, Not Talking Back, Just Talking to Myself, January 1989." *Yearning: Race, Gender, and Cultural Politics*. Ed. bell hooks. Boston: South End Press, 1990. 215–23.

———. *Teaching to Transgress: Education as the Practice of Freedom*. New York: Routledge, 1994.

Hoover, Paul. "South of X." *New American Writing* 14 (1996): 75–86.

Hughes, Langston. "The Weary Blues." *The Norton Anthology of Modern Poetry*. Eds. Richard Ellmann and Robert O'Clair. New York: W. W. Norton & Co., 1973. 635.

Hughes, Robert. *Culture of Complaint: The Fraying of America*. New York: Oxford University Press, 1993.

Huidobro, Vicente. "A Day Will Come" / "Un Dia Vendra." *The Selected Poetry of Vicente Huidobro*. Ed. and trans. David M. Guss. New York: New Directions, 1981. 202–203.

Hurlbert, C. Mark, and Michael Blitz, eds. *Composition and Resistance*. Portsmouth, NH: Boynton/Cook, 1991.

———. "The Institution('s) Lives!" *Pre-text: A Journal of Rhetorical Theory* 13.1–2, Spring/Summer (1992): 59–78.

Hurlbert, C. Mark, and Samuel Totten, eds. *Social Issues in the English Classroom*. Urbana: National Council of Teachers of English, 1992.

Knoblauch, C. H. "Rhetorical Constructions: Dialogue and Commitment." *College English* 50.2 (1988): 125–40.

———. Transcript. In Hurlbert and Blitz. *Composition and Resistance*. 125.

———, and Lil Brannon. *Critical Teaching and the Idea of Literacy*. Portsmouth, NH: Boynton/Cook, 1993.

Jessup, Emily, and Marion Lardner. "Teaching Other People's Children." *Feminine Principles of and Women's Experience in American Composition and Rhetoric*. Eds. Louise Wetherbee Phelps and Janet Emig. Pittsburgh Series in Composition, Literacy, and Culture. Eds. David Bartholomae and Jean Ferguson Carr. Pittsburgh: University of Pittsburgh Press, 1995. 191–210.

Kelly, Robert. *The Loom*. Santa Barbara, CA: Black Sparrow Press, 1975.

Kozol, Jonathan. *Amazing Grace: The Lives of Children and the Conscience of a Nation*. New York: Harper Perennial, 1995.

———. *Savage Inequalities: Children in America's Schools*. New York: Harper Perennial, 1991.

Kruttschnitt, Candace. "Violence by and against Women: A Comparative and Cross-National Analysis." In Ruback and Weiner. 89–108.

Kunstler, James Howard. *The Geography of Nowhere: The Rise and Decline of America's Man-Made Landscape*. New York: Touchstone, 1993.

Linde, Charlotte. *Life Stories: The Creation of Coherence*. New York: Oxford University Press, 1993.

Macrorie, Ken. *Searching Writing*. Upper Montclair, NJ: Boynton/Cook, 1980.

Malinowitz, Harriet. *Textual Orientations: Lesbian and Gay Students and the Making of Discourse Communities*. Portsmouth, NH: Boynton/Cook–Heinemann, 1995.

McAndrew, Donald A., and C. Mark Hurlbert. "Teaching Intentional Errors in Standard English: A Way to 'big smart english.'" *English Leadership Quarterly* 15.2 (1993): 5–7.

McKay, Claude. "If We Must Die." *The Norton Anthology of Modern Poetry*. Eds. Richard Ellmann and Robert O'Clair. New York: W. W. Norton & Co., 1973. 489.

McKibben, Bill. "Reaching the Limit." *The New York Review of Books* 29 May 1997: 32–35.

Montgomery County Student Alliance. "A Student Voice." *Radical School Reform*. Eds. Ronald and Beatrice Gross. New York: Simon & Schuster, 1969. 147–60.

Morris, David B. *The Culture of Pain*. Berkeley: University of California Press, 1991.

Morrison, Toni. *Beloved*. New York: Knopf, 1987.

Muller, Lauren, and the Poetry for the People Collective, eds. *June Jordan's Poetry for the People: A Revolutionary Blueprint*. New York: Routledge, 1995.

Murphy, Ann. "Transference and Resistance in the Basic Writing Classroom: Problematics and Praxis." *College Composition and Communication* 40.2 (1989): 175–87.

The Neighborhoods. "Hate Zone." *Hoodwinked*. Emergo, 1990.

Noddings, Nel. *The Challenge to Care in Schools: An Alternative Approach to Education*. Advances in Contemporary Educational Thought, Vol. 8. Ed. James F. Soltis. New York: Teachers College Press, 1992.

North, Stephen M. *The Making of Knowledge in Composition: Portrait of an Emerging Field*. Upper Montclair, NJ: Boynton/Cook, 1987.

———. Transcript. In Hurlbert and Blitz. *Composition and Resistance*. 125.

O'Reilley, Mary Rose. *The Peaceable Classroom*. Portsmouth, NH: Boynton/Cook–Heinemann, 1993.

Ott, C. Ann, Elizabeth H. Boquet, and C. Mark Hurlbert. "Dinner in the Classroom Restaurant: Sharing a Graduate Seminar." *Sharing Pedagogies: Students and Teachers Write about Dialogic Practices*. Eds. John Tassoni and Gail Tayko. Portsmouth, NH: Boynton/Cook–Heinemann, 1997. 153–76.

Owens, Derek. *Resisting Writings (and the Boundaries of Composition)*. Dallas: Southern Methodist University Press, 1994.

Postman, Neil, and Charles Weingartner. *Teaching as a Subversive Activity*. New York: Dell, 1969.

Prothrow-Smith, Deborah, and Sher Quaday. "Communities, Schools, Violence." In Hoffman. 153–62.

Proust, Marcel. *Remembrance of Things Past: The Past Recaptured*. Trans. Frederick A. Blossom. New York: Random House, 1932.

Rasula, Jed. "The Wax Museum." *The American Poetry Wax Museum: Reality Effects 1940–1990*. Refiguring English Studies. Ed. Stephen M. North. Urbana, IL: National Council of Teachers of English, 1996: 1–56.

Reardon, Betty A. *Comprehensive Peace Education: Education for Global Responsibility*. New York: Teachers College Press, 1988.

———. *Sexism and the War System*. New York: Teachers College Press, 1985.

———, ed. *Women and Peace: Feminist Visions of Global Security*. Global Conflict and Peace Education. Albany, NY: State University of New York Press, 1993.

Readings, Bill. *The University in Ruins*. Cambridge, MA: Harvard UP, 1996.

Reiss, Albert J., and Jeffrey A. Roth, eds. *Understanding and Preventing Violence*. Washington, D.C.: National Academy Press, 1993.

Roddy, Dennis B., "One Dead, One Hurt in IUP Shootings." *Pittsburgh Post-Gazette*. 1 Mar. 1997: A-1, A-5.

Roffman, Rosaly Demaios. "The Poet as Shaker and Healer." *Life on the Line: Selections on Words and Healing*. Eds. Sue Branna Walker and Rosaly Demaios Roffman. Mobile, AL: Negative Capability Press, 1992. 527–45.

Ruback, R. Barry, and Neil Alan Weiner, eds. *Interpersonal Violent Behaviors: Social and Cultural Aspects*. New York: Springer, 1995.

Sanders, Scott Russell. "From Anonymous, Evasive Prose to Writing with Passion." *The Chronicle of Higher Education* 44.7 (10 Oct. 1997): B4–B5.

———. *Writing from the Center*. Bloomington, IN: Indiana University Press, 1995.

Schaafsma, David. *Eating on the Street: Teaching Literacy in a Multicultural Society*. Pittsburgh Series in Composition, Literacy, and Culture. Pittsburgh: University of Pittsburgh Press, 1993.

Smitherman, Geneva. *Talkin and Testifyin: The Language of Black America*. Detroit: Wayne State University Press, 1977.

Somerville, John. *The Philosophy of Peace*. New York: Gaer Associates, 1949.

Stein, Gertrude. "Composition as Explanation." *Selected Writings of Gertrude Stein*. Ed. Carl Van Vechten. New York: Vintage, 1962. 511–23.

Sledd, James. "And They Write Innumerable Books." *Eloquent Dissent: The Writings of James Sledd*. Ed. Richard D. Freed. Portsmouth, NH: Boynton/Cook–Heinemann, 1996. 97–105.

Stuckey, J. Elspeth. *The Violence of Literacy*. Portsmouth, NH: Boynton/Cook, 1991.

Sutton, Sharon E. *Weaving a Tapestry of Resistance: The Places, Power, and Poetry of a Sustainable Society*. Critical Studies in Education and Culture Series. Eds. Henry A. Giroux and Paulo Freire. Westport, CT: Bergin & Garvey, 1996.

Tayko, Gail, and John Tassoni, eds. *Sharing Pedagogies: Students and Teachers Write about Dialogic Practices*. Portsmouth, NH: Boynton/Cook–Heinemann, 1997.

Villanueva, Victor. *Bootstraps: From an American Academic of Color*. Urbana, IL: National Council of Teachers of English, 1993.

Welch, Nancy. *Getting Restless: Rethinking Revision in Writing Instruction*. CrossCurrents: New Perspectives in Composition and Rhetoric. Ed. Charles I. Schuster. Portsmouth, NH: Boynton/Cook–Heinemann, 1997.

Wilson, Margo, and Martin Daly. "An Evolutionary Psychological Perspective on Male Sexual Proprietariness and Violence Against Wives." In Ruback and Weiner. 109–33.

Index

Authors

Michael Blitz (left) lives in Brooklyn, New York, and C. Mark Hurlbert lives in Pittsburgh, Pennsylvania. Hurlbert has co-edited (with Samuel Totten) *Social Issues in the English Classroom*; Blitz has written *Partitions, The Spacialist, Five Days in the Electric Chair*, and *Suction Files*. Together they edited *Composition and Resistance* and have written articles for *Works and Days, Pre/Text, The Writing Instructor, Composition Studies*, and *Discourse*, and book chapters in *Cultural Studies in the English Classroom, Changing Classroom Practices, Social Issues in the English Classroom, Practicing Theory, Getting a Life*, and *Sharing Pedagogies*.

This book was typeset in Palatino and Helvetica by Electronic Imaging.
The typefaces used on the cover were Poppl-Laudatio and Trixie.
The book was printed on 50-lb. Lynx Opaque by IPC Communication Services.